DOUBLE OR NOTHING

Caitlin Press Inc.
8100 Alderwood Road,
Halfmoon Bay, BC V0N 1Y1
www.caitlin-press.com

Edited by Sage Birchwater and Mary Schendlinger
Text and cover design by Michelle Winegar
Uncredited photos are from author's collection.
Printed in Canada

Caitlin Press Inc. acknowledges financial support from the Government of Canada through the Canada Book Fund and the Canada Council for the Arts, and from the Province of British Columbia through the British Columbia Arts Council and the Book Publisher's Tax Credit.

Canada Council   Conseil des Arts
for the Arts   du Canada

BRITISH COLUMBIA
ARTS COUNCIL
We acknowledge the support of the Province of British Columbia through the British Columbia Arts Council

LIBRARY AND ARCHIVES CANADA CATALOGUING IN PUBLICATION
Christensen, Darcy, 1929-
      Double or nothing : the flying fur buyer of Anahim Lake / Darcy Christensen.

ISBN 978-1-894759-47-2

      1. Christensen, Darcy, 1929-. 2. Fur traders—British Columbia—Biography. 3. Bush pilots—British Columbia—Biography. 4. Anahim Lake Region (B.C.)—Biography. 5. Chilcotin River Region (B.C.)—Biography. I. Title.

FC3845.C445C57 2010   971.1'75   C2010-905736-8

DOUBLE OR NOTHING

THE FLYING FUR BUYER OF ANAHIM LAKE

D'ARCY CHRISTENSEN

I WOULD LIKE TO PAY TRIBUTE TO MY COMPANIONS
AND TO THE MAJESTIC MOUNTAINS WE RODE THROUGH OVER THE YEARS,
AND TO THOSE WHO RODE THE TRAILS BEFORE US, SPINNING THE TALES
OF CHILCOTIN AROUND THE CAMPFIRES THAT MARKED OUR WAY.

CONTENTS

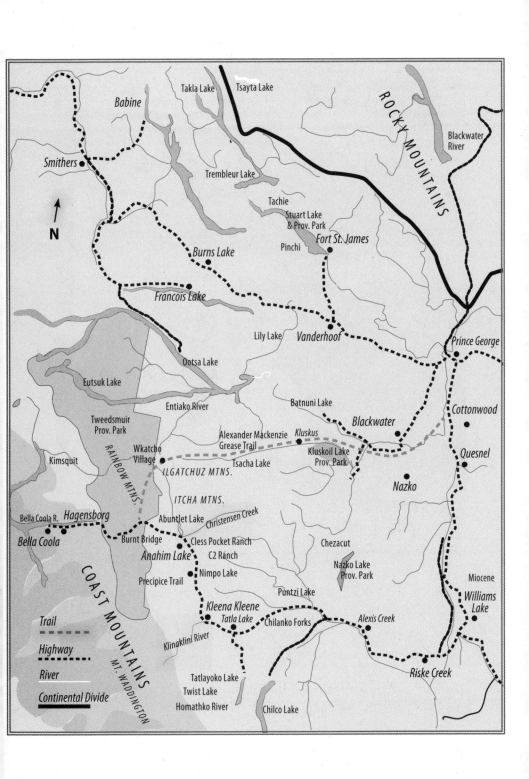

The most exciting trapping experience of my life was nothing new to Thomas Squinas (on the right).

IN THE BEGINNING

I WAS BORN IN 1929 AND I GREW UP IN THE 1930S, IN BELLA COOLA and Anahim Lake. In the winter months we would stay in Bella Coola, where my older sisters Geraldine and Loy and I would go to school and my parents would run the local store.

All us kids had bicycles. The roads were gravel and seemed to be uphill or downhill, and the trails were even worse. I don't know how many spills I had on my bike. Sometimes I would get going too fast down some trail and lose control and go flying off my bike in a crash. Sometimes I would try to slow down by braking and one foot would slip off a pedal and I'd land on the bar between the seat and the steering forks. I'm sure this would bring tears to the eyes of a Brahma bull. When we got a little older, a few of us kids would bicycle up the road about four miles to Thorsen Creek when the salmon were spawning. There would be so many fish in the river it would look like you could walk across the river on their backs.

When we weren't in school, a group of us boys in Bella Coola would be climbing the mountain by the town, riding our bicycles, fishing oolichans with dip nets, or playing on the tide flats. There was always something interesting to keep us busy, and fighting was something we seldom had any interest in. One day a few of us were down on the tide flats loitering around, and I was lying on my back enjoying the sun with my coat half off when Mickey Rasmuson, a boy about my age, took advantage of my vulnerable

Jimmy Holte used to say that there were a lot of ways to kill a cow, but only one way to keep it alive. To keep this motherless calf alive, I teach it a new way to drink milk.

position and pinned me down. For what reason he did this I was never able to determine. He then proceeded to punch my head and face. By the time I was able to break loose from him I was pretty well lumped up.

When I went home for supper that night I must have looked like I had smallpox. My parents were pretty interested in knowing what happened, but not a word was said about the incident. My dad was a hard-working businessman who firmly believed that kids were to be seen and not heard, and my mother never interfered with his directives. After many reprimands I had figured out at a very early age that rules were rules and not to be broken.

One day a few weeks later, a handful of us were out biking on one of the few roads in town when we ran into another group of locals coming in our direction. Mickey Rasmuson was in this group. Everyone knew that Mickey and I had something to settle. We got clear of our bikes, and with diplomacy out of the question, we went at it toe to toe. Two nine- or ten-year-olds may not raise a lot of dust or do a lot of physical damage to each other, but their adrenaline and emotions are at full peak. I had to vindicate myself from our former engagement, and he knew he had a licking coming to him. We fought as hard as we could for what seemed like an eternity. There was no wrestling to this match. It was strictly a punching fest—much too even a fight to suit me. I finally landed a haymaker on his right ear about the same time he gave me a good jab in the chest where I had bruised it in one of my bicycle mishaps. By this time we were both played out and damned glad to quit. Mickey said I had hit him on the ear that had been aching. The fight was pretty much of a draw. We both got favourable comments from the rest of the group, which did a lot for our egos. Mickey and I were pretty sociable to each other after that.

The store that my parents ran had been acquired by my dad, Andy Christensen, from his dad, Adolph, in the 1920s. Adolph came to Bella Coola from Minnesota with the Norwegian colonists

Adolph paid his two oldest sons, Andy and Wilfred, a nickel a board to tear apart the original store on the north side of the valley. Here, the newly rebuilt store (left), is seen next to the Telegraph Building. The Telegraph Building was built out of concrete during World War II.

My dad Andy Christensen (left), with my cousin Pat Ward and my grandfather Adolf. They are standing next to the truck they used for hauling
supplies from Williams Lake.

Front: My grandparents, Adolph and Marit Christensen, Norman is between them, Della has a bow in hair and Wilfred is on the far right. Back: Helmer, Dora, Mike, and my dad Andy. COURTESY PETER SOLHJELL.

in 1894. He started a store in 1898 in the first townsite of Bella Coola, on the north side of the Bella Coola Valley. The river flooded almost yearly, so by the 1920s the settlers were forced to move to the south side of the river. As the road up the valley improved, the local stores followed it, and competition became quite keen. Adolph Christensen, Hagen Christensen (no relation) and Barney Brynildsen all had stores in Hagensborg. Adolph moved his store to the south side of the river in the new Bella Coola townsite after the flood of 1926. He was the first to build on the south side, where the Co-op store is located today. He paid his two oldest sons, Andy and Wilfred, a nickel for each board they tore off the original building to rebuild the new store across the river. Adolph's wife, Marit, owned and ran the Mackenzie Hotel on the south side of the river. Meals were served there until it burned to the ground on July 20, 1944.

Businessmen are a part of my lineage on the other side too. My mother's father, John Clayton, an Englishman, had come to

People exit the Mackenzie Hotel while it burns. The hotel was owned and operated by Adolph's wife, Marit, until it burned down on July 20, 1944.
COURTESY SAGE BIRCHWATER.

the Central Coast of BC in 1873 by boat. He first worked for the Hudson's Bay Company in Bella Bella, and later in Bella Coola, long before the first white settlers arrived. Twice he walked from Vancouver to Bella Coola. In 1874 he got a job working there, and when the postmaster died in 1876 he got the job managing the post. Then the HBC decided to close it down. In 1885 he purchased the lease, and in 1887 he purchased the factor outright. The name of the business remained the Hudson's Bay Factor. In the deal he got the land on the south side of the

John Clayton was my grandfather, the earliest white settler in Bella Coola and the owner of the last Hudson's Bay outpost in the valley.
COURTESY PETER SOLHJELL.

In the early 1900s, travel to and from Bella Coola was done by boat. Mrs. Clayton (second from right) is shown here aboard one of the ferries.

Bella Coola River from the tide flats almost to the Tatsquam River to the east, and to the mountains on the south side, where the Bella Coola townsite is today. John died in 1910, and his wife Elizabeth ran the business for years afterward.

I don't remember ever hearing John Clayton's name mentioned around home, so years later I dug up more information as I could find it in various books. Clayton was no doubt a pretty astute businessman and acquired a fair amount of wealth in his day. He apparently owned a steamship and used it in his business between Victoria, Bella Coola and Bella Bella. He and Tom Draney, one of Bella Coola's first settlers, built a fish cannery near the townsite. Clayton had the money and Draney had the expertise. Clayton's trading business with the local Natives was well established when the first settlers arrived, so his business would have thrived.

It is odd that I never heard Clayton's name mentioned—not a word about him, even though he was my grandfather. Over time I learned that he was supposed to have lived with a Native lady from the Bella Coola reserve and sired a son, Willie Mack. In those days

The Clayton house was built on the south bank of the Bella Coola River and had spacious rooms for entertaining and feeding the early, hungry settlers.

an Englishman who married out of his class was frowned upon. Many Englishmen came to Canada, got established and then went back to England to marry. Because of this custom I missed a lot of history. John Clayton eventually did go back to England to find a wife. He married my grandmother, Elizabeth Clayton, a minister's daughter much younger than himself, and brought her back to Bella Coola. She was the first white woman in Bella Coola and was always invited to the potlatches. She wore her hair all trussed up in a bun. Those were the days of big skirts, and the little children at the potlatches would hide under her skirt when they got frightened by the dancers. I don't remember my grandmother too well, because she retired to Victoria when I was quite young. But I do remember that Mrs. Clayton used to send rolls of funny papers addressed to me at Anahim Lake.

With both parents and both sets of grandparents running businesses, it's no wonder I became an entrepreneur too. Something in my genes, maybe.

Schooling in Bella Coola was probably on par with the rest of the province in the lower grades. Grades one through six were taught in a one-room school by one teacher. Seven miles up the valley, grades seven through twelve were taught in the same manner. In grade seven we had a staunch Communist teacher who had three or four favourite pupils and didn't care if the rest of us learned anything or not. I wasn't one of the favourites, and it was a wasted year. By that time I was playing a lot of poker in the evenings. The school was heated by a barrel wood stove in the winter, and I was so tired from my evening poker exploits that the heater would soon put me to sleep. In this state I was much more able to endure the year. Grade eight brought a different teacher and an improvement in learning.

In 1945 I had the opportunity to go to Victoria for grade nine. There was a school across the street from where I was staying, so I went to it. The school was called St. Louis College. I had unknowingly picked a Catholic school run by brothers. This school woke me up to learning. I took algebra, geometry, French, Latin, chemistry, social studies and history. We got three hours of homework a night and the teachers made sure it was done. One day my chemistry teacher quizzed me on the homework. His first question was: What is a catalyst? I didn't know, so he had me write down fifty times that a catalyst is a substance that changes the speed of a chemical reaction without itself being permanently changed. I had to do it on my own time that night. Sixty-five years later I still remember. He was one damned fine teacher. It's a shame public schools today

My grade nine class at St. Louis College in Victoria BC. I'm kneeling, second from the right, and look proud that I'd had a fairly productive year.

Tommy Walker's outfit starts out along Bella Coola Road in 1948 to the Spatsizi. This nine-hundred-mile trek goes through the coastal mountains, then north to the headwaters of the Stikine River. COURTESY SAGE BIRCHWATER.

don't teach like they did at St. Louis College, but without all the Hail Marys that went along with it.

Every summer when school was out, our parents would move us all to my dad's cattle ranch in Anahim Lake, about a hundred miles east of Bella Coola, by horseback. All supplies for the ranch were taken as far up the valley as a vehicle could be driven, about forty-five miles, to what was then the end of the road. From there, at the trailhead, we'd be met by a couple of men who worked on the ranch. My dad would have arranged for them to bring the necessary number of packhorses to take the family and supplies to the ranch, about fifty-five miles away. The trail ran through the Coast Mountains to the high Chilcotin Plateau country, rising from about sea level to four thousand feet. We followed switchbacks on the steepest mountain grades to lessen the incline, but it was still a grunt for the horses. The trip took three days, a lot of it through jackpine, but there was some beautiful mountain scenery as well.

We would pass the odd small lake and there always seemed to be a couple of loons singing their haunting cry as we went by.

Anahim Lake refers to the town of Anahim Lake as well as the lake itself, and sometimes to the immediate surrounding area. The east end of the lake is squeezed in size and depth and is called Little Anahim Lake. The town is built on the east end of Little Anahim but just far enough away so the lake is not visible from the town. My dad's ranch was called Cless Pocket Ranch, a name that means "white mud" in the local aboriginal language. One of the pastures on the ranch had a large area of alkali on it, which is the white the Natives called Cless Pocket.

♠

In the spring of the year, when the grass had started to grow, Andy would have about thirty head of beef cattle driven down the hill from Anahim Lake to Bella Coola to be butchered for the store. He would have them pastured on the Bella Coola tide flats west of town, and he would butcher two animals a week. Without refrigeration, the meat had to be sold quickly. Andy's younger brother, Wilfred, said that in the early 1930s he used to grind twenty-four pounds of hamburger by hand every morning before eight o'clock when the store opened. The hamburger sold for 12 cents a pound, and T-bone steaks were 18 cents a pound. The meat business became much easier in 1935, when Andy acquired a gas-powered refrigerator unit that kept the meat at 32 degrees Fahrenheit.

Wilfred, who had been store manager for Andy, said the store had a wide variety of goods. He once sold a Marconi radio to Dr. McLean, a very religious man who ran the Bella Coola hospital for the United Church. Upon hooking up the radio and turning it on, the first thing the good doctor heard was a hymn being sung. I guess he was thrilled with his purchase.

♠

My preference between Bella Coola and the Cless Pocket Ranch showed up early in my life. One day a school pal, Sydney Brynildsen, and I decided to walk to Anahim Lake. For sustenance on the long journey we took a few chocolate-covered hard candies.

Horses at Cless Pocket were well fed by plentiful crops. COURTESY SAGE BIRCHWATER.

I guess nobody paid any attention to us as we walked along. Most houses were built well back from the road and nobody would have noticed us anyway. Eventually it got dark and we were missed at home. My dad got the only policeman in the valley, a man by the name of Condon, to go with him in search of the two missing boys. They drove up the road, as that would be the most likely direction we'd have taken. By this time, when Sydney and I would hear a car coming we would grab Sydney's little spaniel that we had taken with us and duck off the road into the bush. But on one occasion we didn't grab the dog quick enough, and the car stopped. The two occupants of the car, my dad and Constable Condon, got out and Condon said, "You can come out now, the game is up." I can still hear his words, and he was right. Sydney and I never tried that again. We had made it twelve miles with about eighty-eight to go.

Throughout my school years I always spent the summer holidays working on the ranch. The number one priority was putting up hay for feed for the cattle and other stock. We did the haying with horse-drawn implements, mowers, rakes and slips. The hay slips were eight-by-twelve-foot platforms on two wooden runners pulled by two horses. Slings were placed on the platform before loading it with hay. The slings were divided into two parts, hooked together by a mechanism that could be tripped by the stacker. The slips were loaded by hand with pitchforks and pulled to a central stacking area where derrick poles had been put up to stack the hay. These poles were fifty or sixty feet long and were erected in an up-side-down *V.* They were anchored by cables tied to the tops of the poles and to stakes driven into the ground in front of and behind the poles. These cables were adjusted so the poles swung forward when the load of hay was pulled up and off the slip. This was done by other cables that had two blocks on them to hook into rings on each end of the slings. When the load cleared the slip, the poles would swing back to where the stack was being built. The stacker would grab a short rope that had been coiled under the slings and use it to trip the sling and place the load where he wanted it.

To feed several hundred head of cattle, a hundred sheep and a few workhorses, a lot of hay was required. Most of the horses

This haying device was called a slide stacker. Using hay sweeps, we would move hay onto the lower part, hoist it up then drop it onto a stack below.

rustled all winter. Everybody on the crew worked hard in those days. There was just no room for shirkers. At least half the crew were Natives, a happy bunch who did a lot of whooping and hollering coming to work and going back again. It was a great environment for a young man like me to work in. In haying season you started at seven in the morning unless it was your turn to wrangle the horses. Then it would be five. We'd have a cold lunch in the middle of the day, right in the field where we were working. We'd quit at six in the evening, and when suppertime came around, everybody was damned hungry.

My mother always cooked for the crew, and she was an excellent cook. She built meals around moose meat, as moose were in plentiful supply. In later years, sheep became the main staple. A sheep would last about four days. There was no refrigeration, but when it was hung in a cool meat shed that was fly-proofed, the mutton kept fine. Desserts were usually pies and cakes.

Haying required big crews and horse-drawn equipment, so it didn't always proceed without incident. One day before the Second World War, my uncle Vinnie Clayton was cutting hay on one of the meadows with a horse-drawn mower. Another worker was on a mower cutting behind him. Something spooked the horses. The team behind Vinnie ran into the back of his mower and knocked him off his machine, and he fell in front of his sickle bar. His team must have jumped forward, and the cutting bar cut one of Vinnie's legs off and badly cut the other. Vinnie somehow hung onto the reins of his team and was able to wrap a rein around his leg and get the bleeding under control.

Jane Lehman, a local nurse and the one and only medical personnel in the country, was called in and took charge of Vinnie. She got a makeshift stretcher made and had Vinnie carried to the Cless Pocket Ranch headquarters, about three miles away. My dad, Andy, wired for an airplane but the weather was unflyable. Jane spent the night cleaning Vinnie's wounds, which were full of dirt and grass. Rich Hobson, who happened by that day, helped her. With the simple tools Jane had to work with, she did a remarkable job.

For years Grandpa Adolph was the handyman on the ranch. Here is a regal photograph of him with the original ranch house in the background.

My grandfather, Adolph, phoned Andy from Bella Coola to arrange to have horses meet him and the Bella Coola doctor at Stuie. Billy Dagg met them, and after a hard night's riding they arrived at the Cless Pocket Ranch. Dr. Phillips immediately saw that Jane had done all that could be done and he, Billy and Adolph went to bed. The next day the plane arrived and flew Vinnie and the doctor to Vancouver, where Vinnie healed up amazingly quickly. He made a complete recovery, minus one leg. Jane had put the stump of his severed leg into a sack of flour, and that had stopped the bleeding and saved his life.

After graduating from high school in Bella Coola in 1947, I worked one winter in the paper mill in Powell River, then spent one winter in Victoria taking a business course at Sprott-Shaw. Then I started working steady on the ranch.

When haying was finished in the fall, the crew was cut down to me, Bob Smith, Bob Draney and Gordon Wilson. My dad ran the store on the ranch and left the ranching pretty much to the hired help. To make the jobs more attractive, the main hands were allowed to run a few head of their own cattle on the ranch. Some of the men who started ranching on their own by this method were Billy Dagg, Tommy Holte, John Clayton, Bob Draney and me. For many years, the cattle were driven to market in Williams Lake. Bob Smith was usually the head man on these drives, which took about twenty-four days.

In 1939 the local ranchers decided to take their beef to Bella Coola and then to Vancouver by barge. Gulf of Georgia Towing, the contractor, fixed up a scow with feeding mangers and pens with watering facilities for the estimated number of cattle that would be brought from Anahim Lake. Corrals were built on the tide flats so that the cattle could be loaded. In the fall of 1939, a drive of 110 head took off from Anahim Lake, with Tim Draney, Thomas Squinas, Billy Dagg, Victor Brink and Alfred Bryant as cowboys. The drive went down the Dean River, then up the Ulkatcho pack trail (Alexander Mackenzie Grease Trail), through the Rainbow Mountains and down into Bella Coola Valley at Burnt Bridge. Two of the

Laurena and Tim Draney, with Tommy Holte and Lester Dorsey. Stopping for a bite to eat on the trail.

Going on a moose hunt (L to R): Thomas Squinas, Skeeter McCraken (who came all the way from California), Jeannie and Dave Dorsey, and Nestor Malinsky.

cattle fell off the trail going down the mountain, but these were the only animals lost on the trip. The drive took twelve days. The next year, 1940, Gulf of Georgia Towing wanted more money, so the drive was discontinued.

As the road between Anahim Lake and Williams Lake slowly improved, it became more difficult to drive a herd of cattle along it. Vehicle traffic had increased, and the gravel put down on the roadway damaged the cattle's hooves. The last drives went east from Anahim Lake past Sugarloaf Mountain and came out close to Puntzi on the highway. From Puntzi they were trucked to Williams Lake. I went on two of the drives to Puntzi. On beef drives, cattle are moved slowly and are pampered along the way so they don't lose weight by getting heated up or fatigued. The Puntzi drive took a week, and to me it seemed like a vacation. It was the first time I had been on a drive, and it was a change from the normal fall work, and I got to see a lot of new country.

A muddy Chilcotin Road before World War II. At this time, the trip from Williams Lake to Anahim Lake took days instead of hours.

Eventually, as the roads got much better and trucks got bigger, cattle drives from Anahim Lake were phased out entirely. Elton Elliot built one of the main cattle hauling businesses in the Chilcotin. He didn't always have the best equipment in the world, and on one trip from Anahim Lake to Williams Lake with a load of cattle, Tommy Engebretson, the driver, had seven flat tires. How he finally made it to Williams Lake I don't know. When asked by someone how the job was going, he said: "Well, sometimes it gets pretty exciting you know."

Tommy was right about cattle hauling. On the Cless Pocket Ranch we had a truck for freighting supplies to the ranch as well as hauling cattle to market, and I once used it to take a load of cattle to Williams Lake, late in the fall when the road from Riske Creek to Williams Lake was very icy. I slid off a turn at Riske Creek but was stopped pretty quickly when I nudged a big rock sticking out of the snow. The icy patch seemed like an isolated section of the

These men make navigating a Nuxalt canoe raft look easy, but it is not. I once watched a one-armed Native man pole a canoe all the way across the river. I learned a great deal from these resourceful men and women.

road, so I continued without putting the chains on. I proceeded down Sheep Creek Hill without any trouble, until I got to Cape Horn. I don't know how this part of the road got its name, but at that time it had an 18-percent grade. I began to crawl down it in my lowest gear, and I had just started down the steep decline when I hit some glare ice. The truck took off like it was on skis, went a short distance and then hit dirt again. By this time the truck was going much too fast for the gear I was in, and I thought when the wheels caught and started to turn the engine, that engine was going to blow up. But except for making a deafening roar, the motor was not harmed. When I got to the last climb up the Williams Lake hill, the road was plugged with vehicles getting chains put on. I pulled over and started putting my chains on. I had the job pretty well done when a driver in a truck coming down the hill yelled out to clear the road, as he didn't think he could hold his truck back any longer. His tires must have heated up and started slipping. Everyone gave him room. With chains on, the rest of the trip wasn't nearly as exciting.

I learned something about fishing from the Native people I got to know when I was young, especially Joe Grambush, from the Chilcotin country, and Old Baptiste Stillas, from Ulkatcho Village. On one of our pack-train trips up the Atnarko River Valley to Anahim Lake when I was a boy, Joe was one of the packers. We camped for the night not far from the river, and after supper Joe got a pole with a gaff on it that apparently had been left by the river. I was pretty interested to know how he was going to get a fish out of that river. All I could see was fast-moving water over the rocks on the bottom. But before long, Joe made a sudden move with the pole and had a twenty-pound spring salmon. The gaff was tied to the pole with a piece of rope, and it was designed to come loose when it snagged a fish. The fish was hanging from the end of the pole as Joe quickly brought it to shore.

On the Cless Pocket Ranch, I went with Joe down the creek that ran through the property, called Christensen Creek. This time he was after suckers. He had a ten- or twelve-foot pole and had anchored a hook on it made out of a nail. When he ran into a school of spawning suckers, he easily hooked several and flipped them up on the bank. Joe made fishing look easy, but I knew he was just damned skilful. This guy would never go hungry.

We used to have a dam at the head of two hay meadows on either side of Christensen Creek. The dam was built so we could put boards into it to back up water for irrigation. Old Stillas eyed this up one day when it wasn't being used, and the next thing we knew he had put a box in the creek where it ran through the dam. The back of the box extended vertically, and when a trout tried to jump up through the fast-moving water, it would hit the back of the box and fall back into the box. Old Stillas was another fellow who wasn't going to go hungry.

Before computers and automation, milling was mostly muscle and horse
power. Lester and I show how it's done.

♠ LESTER DORSEY

Lester Dorsey came from Washington State in the early 1920s and settled in the Tatlayoko Valley. Over a few drinks at one of our gatherings, I once heard him sing a kind of homemade song about being down in the Homathko. From Tatlayoko he made his way to Anahim Lake, where he got a job packing for the Hudson's Bay Company. The HBC had a store in Anahim Lake and they packed the goods for the store over the Precipice Trail from Bella Coola. Bob Bowser ran this trading post for a number of years, and through his son Edwin he must have many grandchildren in the Williams Lake area.

Lester married Mickey Tuck from Bella Coola. Mickey's dad was a ship carpenter from Nova Scotia, not very big in stature but pretty fiery. He did some carpentering on my dad's second cabin at the Cless Pocket Ranch and had a reputation for doing meticulous work. I was at the age to have more fun doing something a little bit naughty than exactly right, so I went into the cabin where he was working, and when he went into another room I banged a piece of wood on one of the logs like I was hammering something. He was back in the room so fast I almost literally had to fly out of there to escape his wrath.

Lester was a rugged six feet tall with no fat, and hands shaped from years of axe work and packing horses. I always thought his fingernails must be strong enough to punch holes in a milk can, and perhaps contained enough bacteria for biological warfare. He would get a piece of meadowland close to Anahim Lake, build a log cabin on it to live in, build fences and corrals, get a passable way into the property, ranch on it for two or three years, then sell it and move to another location and start all over again. He started ranching at a place called Trail's End, southwest of Anahim Lake. From there he moved to the west side of Anahim Lake. After a few years on these two places he moved east of Anahim Lake. The places he owned or used in his ranching operations were Trail's End, Two-Mile, Three-Mile, Four-Mile and

Big Meadow, plus all the open range he needed.

While Lester was building ranches and packing freight, he also got into the guiding business. Mickey was very busy raising five boys, Fred, Mike, Frank, Steve and Dave, and one daughter, Wanda. Another son, Kenny, had died as a child. I wouldn't have wanted to wrestle any of Lester's boys. They were a pretty sturdy bunch. Lester and Mickey did their work and raised their family without the benefits of modern conveniences. No running water, no washing machines, no indoor toilets and of course no disposable diapers. In those days most of the moving was done by horses and sleigh, or team and wagon. In the winter, temperatures often fell to 60 below.

Mickey also worked as a schoolteacher. She taught me correspondence in grade five. When her children got older, she taught in schools farther afield, as far east as Miocene and other places near Williams Lake. It has often been said that life in Anahim Lake was hard on horses and women. It doesn't take much thinking to understand why. Mickey was one of the pioneering women who bore the hardships without complaining. In fact, I'm sure she enjoyed her life.

My first recollections of Lester come from my days as a kid on the Cless Pocket Ranch. He would sometimes stay the night when he arrived late looking for cattle or whatever. Being an early riser he would sometimes cook breakfast. The original ranch house was a long, narrow series of rooms. The first room had the cookstove and a long table that would seat a lot of eaters. The next room was used to keep the cooking ingredients, buckets of water and so on. The bedrooms were beyond these two rooms. Lester usually cooked hotcakes, so he would make many trips back and forth from the stove to the room where we kept the sack of flour and other things he needed. My mother said when she got on the scene, she could tell how close breakfast was to being ready by the trail of flour Lester had left on the floor. Lester may not have been the tidiest cook in the world but I don't remember any complaints about his cooking.

Many a yarn was spun by these two characters—Lester and Pan Phillips—over a social drink or two.

Lester and I crossed paths quite frequently. I took my first trip to the Itcha Mountains with him. We encountered two or three caribou at one point, and he decided to see how close he could get to them on his saddle horse. The horse was willing but the caribou had little trouble disappearing over the next ridge.

Lester, Bob Cohen, Evan Sleeman and I rode into the Itchas one year. Evan had owned the Cless Pocket Ranch for a while, and Bob Cohen looked after the cattle a group of us ranchers used to range in the Itcha Mountains. We left the Itchas and rode straight over to the Ilgachuz Mountains to the west, with the intention of hitting the Blackwater Trail and following it south to Anahim Lake. When we got to the Ilgachuz, visibility had dropped to near zero and we crossed the trail without realizing it. We finally made a circle and came back to it. The packhorses and saddle horses were confused. Lester got a call of nature, and by the time he got back and we were ready to ride, none of us knew which direction Anahim Lake was. Bob and Lester had both spent their lives in the bush, and I had spent a lot of time in it. The Blackwater was to the north, Anahim Lake was to the south, this we knew. But which way was which, we had no idea. After much discussion, Bob found the solution. He got enough light out of the overcast to make a vague shadow with his knife. He then figured out where the sun would be at that time of day, which of course was south, and we were on our way.

Lester had a sawmill of sorts, which he ran with his big Ford tractor. By this time I had bought some property at Corkscrew Creek and I had some good spruce growing there, so we decided to cut lumber one winter. Lester did the falling and I did the limbing and skidding with my team of horses. Once when I appeared a little nervous skidding when he was falling, Lester told me a good faller always looks after his skidder man. I thanked him profusely but said I would still keep both eyes open. I used the team to skid the logs to where Lester could get them with the tractor, and he would skid them to where we were going to set up his mill. By early spring, when it was warm enough to mill the logs, we had finished logging.

I had hardly ever seen a sawmill before. My job was to shovel the sawdust, pack the slabs, pile the lumber and keep the logs ready to be rolled to the saw. Everything I did seemed to be an uphill struggle. When we finally got a wagonload of boards, we took it to Harold Engebretson's because Lester owed him a load. I guess this first load suffered from the set-up changes and adjustments of getting the mill ready. When we loaded the lumber, some of it looked pretty wedgy. Later, Harold told someone about the lumber and said, "You know, someone could have got hurt cutting lumber like that."

I used the team around the mill to pull in logs that couldn't be rolled onto the cutting carriage on the mill. By this time my team and I only operated in high gear. When I yelled, they were on their toes. On one trip when I was coming back from dropping off a log with the doubletree and chain in tow, the horses were chomping on the bit when we got to the skid road. I had to really move to keep up with them. My leather gloves were wet and the reins were wet. Lester was walking down the skid road when I tripped on a limb on the ground, and the reins slipped out of my grasp. I just had time to yell a warning to Lester. The horses ran on either side of him as he ducked down, and the doubletree hit a bump and went over top of him without touching him. When I asked Lester if he was all right, he said he was. "But I mean, I sat on something sharp." Luck sometimes plays a big hand in our lives. The team had run into some tall brush that fouled the bridle lines and they were forced to stop. Work went on as usual, but it was quite a while before I could erase the thought of what the outcome would have been if the doubletree hadn't made such a miraculous bounce over top of Lester and hit him in the back instead.

Lester often inserted "I mean" into his conversation, whether it made sense or not. Once when he was pondering how people grow old and eventually die, he said, "You know when a man starts taking short steps, I mean, you know he hasn't got long to go." Adolph Schilling, a friend of his who had a small ranch not far away, had died. Schilling had been a dentist in Norway and also a top skier in his prime. How he wound up in Anahim Lake is anybody's guess. When Lester broke the news after Schilling died, he said, "And he died prostitute too, I mean."

Our sawmill set-up was within easy walking distance from my house, so Lester and I used to walk home to eat the lunch that my wife, Judy, had prepared for us. Sometimes Lester would complain about not feeling well and would lie out in the sun and rest after lunch. This happened on several occasions. Later he found out that he was probably having a bout with kidney stones, which would have been a miserable thing to work with.

As spring wore on, we gradually got all the logs cut up into boards. Lester seemed to have got things lined up a little better in the mill after the load we had hauled to Harold's, and the lumber looked much better to me. I think we were cutting on a free cutting permit through Forestry. In those days nobody paid much attention to what was happening in Anahim Lake. So we hauled the lumber to my dad's store in Anahim Lake and eventually sold it.

Lester always had a pair of goggles hanging around his neck when cutting lumber. The goggles were to protect his eyes from anything flying back when the saw was working, but he told me he didn't wear them because he could blink fast enough. On taking one load of boards to town, I told him he should take his goggles so we would look more like mill operators. Sure enough, he thought it was a good idea and perched them high on his forehead, and we delivered a load to the store like two seasoned mill operators.

In the Ilgatchuz mountains (L to R): Dad, me (with gun), Billy Dagg and his wife Margaret nee Bowser. In the foreground is their first child, George.

We didn't make a fortune, but we got grubstaked for a while. With a little spending money it was certainly an interesting winter for me. If Lester ever had a spare moment, he liked nothing better than to BS someone over a cup of coffee, spinning yarns about what he was doing or going to do or had done. The topic could go from horses to hunting to travelling in the mountains, to anything else having to do with the outdoors. Time passed very quickly.

When Lester didn't have a group of hunters to associate with, he would often run into some man in town who would strike his fancy, and bring him back to the ranch. It might be a good axe man, builder, mechanic, or what-have-you. In this way he would have someone new to talk to as well as getting some help building or fixing machinery. His screening process for those people wasn't a hundred percent effective, though. One day when a visitor of Lester's was staying on the ranch, I was talking to Mickey, and the man's name came up in our conversation and Mickey told me she loathed him. I remember this because *loathe* is such a powerful word, and I have hardly ever heard it used. For her sake, I hope his stay was short-lived.

One of the good characters that Lester introduced to the country was Slim Mackey. He became a famous log builder and eventually published a book on the subject and started his own log-building school. I saw him at the wedding of Lester and Mickey's grand-daughter, Punky. The wedding was held out on an open flat below the main ranch headquarters. There was an old abandoned cabin on it that Slim had stayed in many years before. It was winter, he said, and you could look out the window any time and see moose on the flat.

The hunters that Lester guided probably came up to see him as much as to hunt. They had a chance to be out in the wilderness with a living frontiersman—a rugged individual who drew blood every time he shaved, left a small sample of any meal he had eaten in the corners of his mouth or on his chin, and was a disaster eating corn on the cob. To go out in the wilderness with him for a week or ten days must have been the highlight of the year for many of these men. The game they hunted was usually in good supply, and if they needed a little pick-me-up in the evening, there would always be room on a packhorse for a few bottles. Something interesting would be happening from morning until night.

One hunter who came back from one of these trips could hardly wait to tell of his adventures. He said that on the first morning in camp he noticed there was no toilet paper. Not wanting to be seen as a softie among the guides and other hunters, he asked no questions, but he was pretty curious as to what he could use as a substitute. He soon noticed that a handful of moss seemed to work well. By the next morning they had climbed higher in the mountains and there was no moss at that altitude. Fortunately he saw that anything salvaged from small jackpines would do the job. The next morning they were camped in mostly shale rock, so no TP choices were available. "If we had climbed any higher," the hunter said, "I know Lester would have used a cloud."

Lester and Mickey raised their boys in an environment of hard work and not much chance for a lot of schooling. Their son Dave once told me that if you weren't a man by the time you were fifteen,

Lester was like me: The older he got, the more he liked horses. PHOTO
HANK WINNING.

you would never be a man. He said that one fall he was working for his dad, guiding moose hunters in the Itcha Mountains. The hunters had filled out their quotas and Lester and Dave packed the moose onto packhorses and started the long trek out of the mountains. Lester was known as a man who usually got going someplace in the "shank of the evening." So here was Dave, fifteen years old, looking after a bunch of dudes and several head of packhorses loaded with moose in the gathering darkness, and Lester riding on ahead, exploring, probably focussed on the country he would be riding through and was so fond of. It wouldn't occur to him that it would be a problem to leave a fifteen-year-old with that responsibility.

Lester died in 1982, at the age of seventy-eight. As Paul St. Pierre wrote, "The winds of time ran out on Lester." A legend had passed with little chance of a successor, as the environment that had shaped Lester's character had also passed on.

♠ DOMAS SQUINAS

One of the first old-time Indians I knew was Chief Domas Squinas. He was a fairly old man when I met him at the Cless Pocket Ranch. He had stopped in to chat with us or have a coffee. I was seven or eight years old and had a .22 calibre pump-action gun that I was very proud of owning. Domas and I were sitting on a plain homemade couch and I of course had to show him how my old .22 worked. This gun had a bad habit of retaining a shell when you thought you had emptied it, a fact that hadn't imprinted itself on my mind quite yet.

I showed Domas how the hand pump worked and how a shell would go into the breach of the gun and be ready to fire with just a single movement of the pump. I knew that you never pointed a gun at anything you didn't want to shoot, so I had the gun pointed down at what we were sitting on. During my second demonstration of how my "empty" gun worked, I shot a bullet into the seat between us. Domas was fairly cool. He just laughed and said: "Pretty near you shoot my ass putat." *Putat* was a term that he and only he used, as far as I know.

One time Domas got on the receiving end of a moose. The story goes that he was hunting up in the Ilgachuz Mountains with his grandson, Little Thomas, and wounded a moose. The moose attacked him and did a lot of damage to him with its front feet. Domas later died from the effects of this encounter. I remember watching a big dog we had at Cless Pocket keep a moose at bay under a jackpine tree. The moose would go after the dog, striking at it with its front feet. The dog easily got out of its way and when the moose turned to run, the dog would lunge in after the moose's hind hocks. Neither the moose nor the dog was going to get anywhere, and the dog was finally called off. Domas wasn't so lucky. He must have gotten off his horse to shoot the moose. He was an old man at that time, and once on the ground he didn't have much chance of getting away from the moose.

When Domas first lived at Anahim Lake reserve with his family, he was the only Ulkatcho inhabitant on the reserve. He also had a house in Ulkatcho Village, about fifty miles away down the Dean River, where most of the rest of the Natives lived. Domas trapped

Old Francis Cassam (the Native "witch doctor"), Louis Squinas and Tom Baptiste. Francis was respected by the community for his healing abilities.

Thomas Squinas, one of Domas's sons, was a famous wolf hunter employed by the government.

PHOTO SAGE BIRCHWATER.

and traded for fur, and he must have done pretty well because he raised the fastest string of saddle horses in the West Chilcotin. When I was a kid I heard stories of Domas making "peaches wine" and, after a certain amount had been consumed, getting on one of his fine horses and seeing how fast he could make it run to the Sulins' place at Fish Trap, a distance of at least nine miles. It must have been an exhilarating run.

Domas and his wife Christine raised three boys, Louie, Donald and Thomas, and one daughter, Balonic. After Domas died, Louie became the hereditary chief. (Elections of chiefs came later.) Louie lived at the west end of Anahim Lake, west of Abuntlet Lake. He built his living quarters on the Dean River where it exited Anahim Lake on its wild journey to Kimsquit and the Pacific Ocean.

Louie was noted for his sense of humour. He was very proud of his lineage in becoming chief, but this didn't stop him from seeing the funny side of things. When the doctor gave him a shot of penicillin in the hind end for a toothache, he told him, "My ass he no sick; my tooth he sick." And when anyone asked him how he was doing, he always responded with the same reply: "What the matter you? I'm good man still. Two times a night yet. Huh, huh, huh!"

Louie raised a nice herd of cattle on his ranch with his wife, Josephine. They raised two boys, Jimmy and Oggie, and one daughter, Bella. Jimmy accidentally shot himself at an early age and died of the wound. Years later the same thing happen to

Oggie where he was living in the Bella Coola Valley.

When I was very young, Louie got the job of holding down the fort with me for a couple of hours one afternoon on one of his visits to the Cless Pocket Ranch. I guess it didn't take me too long to display more energy than he liked. He spied a spud sack on the floor and picked it up for me to see and said, "You be good or I put you sack. Huh, huh, huh!" For Louie I was a quick learner and never got the sack treatment, but he kidded me for years afterward about putting me in a sack.

Lucy Sulin was Willie Sulin's wife and a half-sister to both Billy Dagg and Thomas Squinas's wife, Celestine. .

The last time I saw Louie was in the old folks' home in Williams Lake. He shared a room with Bill Christie, the former Indian agent. I hadn't seen either of them for quite a while. The first thing Louie brought up was the story about his tooth. "Huh, huh, huh!" His sense of humour lasted to the end.

Domas's son Thomas Squinas married Celestine Dagg, a half-sister of Billy Dagg and Lucy Dagg (Sulin), and raised one son and a bevy of beautiful daughters. Thomas's main hay meadow was on the west side of Anahim Lake, and his living quarters were on Corkscrew Creek, east of the lake and two miles north of the town of Anahim Lake. At these two places the Squinas family raised sheep, cattle and the horses they needed for trapping and hunting. In Thomas's day, wolves were the scourge of the area, and the government hired him to get the wolf population under control. He got a bonus for each set of ears he turned in, and he became the most famous wolf hunter in the country. He hunted and trapped them, and he poisoned them by putting out bait laced with strychnine on the frozen lakes. How many wolves he killed I don't think he kept track of, but it was in the hundreds. He told me he had once come upon a pack of wolves feeding on a kill northwest of Cless Pocket, and was able to shoot several of them before the pack had a chance to run off.

One winter when I was very young, one of our bulls died in the feeding area. The carcass was dragged into the brush alongside the meadow below the corrals and house, and Thomas was asked if he could catch some of the coyotes that were always a menace to the sheep we had. I went with him when he set the traps. He found the main trails that the coyotes had made to feed on the carcass, and I will never forget how carefully he placed and covered the traps so the coyotes would step right in them without getting spooked away. When Thomas and I checked the traps the next morning, he had caught two coyotes. This was probably old hat to him, but it was the most exciting trapping experience I had ever had.

When plans to build the road to Bella Coola got underway, Thomas was hired to scout out and flag where it should go, since he hunted and guided in the area and knew it so well. It is Thomas who is responsible for the route Highway 20 follows today, from Anahim Lake to the top of the Bella Coola Hill.

Domas's daughter, Belonic, married Casimer Alexis from the Blackwater, and they had three children, Lena (Capoose), Theresa (Holte) and Albert Casimer. After Casimer died, Belonic married Ollie Nukalow and had one daughter, Vivian (Cahoose), with him. Belonic died of tuberculosis at Behind Meadow, a part of Cless Pocket Ranch, during haying season. Besides raising a large family with Peter Cahoose, Vivian became the elected chief of the Ulka-tcho people during the 1970s. This was quite fitting, since her family had been the last of the hereditary chiefs.

ON MY OWN

THE CLESS POCKET RANCH CONTROLLED ABOUT 3,600 ACRES OF land through leases and Crown grant. In addition we had several hundred acres of grazing leases. There was always lots to do to keep things running. After the hay was put up, stackyards had to be moose-proofed, miles of fence had to be maintained and an endless supply of firewood had to be cut. For years this was done without the benefit of chainsaws.

I worked on the ranch from 1950 to 1959. By then I had built up a modest herd of my own cattle, which I moved to a small acreage of land at Corkscrew Creek that my dad had given me, and there, in 1960, I started ranching on my own. I built a small log cabin that was quite comfortable. While I was batching I could cook eggs, bacon and toast, and make coffee on top of an airtight heater. It's amazing what the stomach can put up with.

A large family, the Brecknocks, had moved to Alexis Creek. They were originally from Quebec and had come to the area via North Vancouver. The family included Stan and Ann and their six children, Slim, Don, John, Toni, Susan and Judy. I met up with Judy at the Anahim Lake Stampede in the late 1950s and we were married in North Vancouver.

After our wedding we went back to my place in Anahim Lake to live. We had three kids, Cary, Chuck and Andrea. The house got too small, so I built a large addition onto it. For Judy it must have

Judy came from the big city to the sticks of Anahim Lake, where the nearest neighbour was only "two swamps away" (as stated by Zeke Bryant).

been quite a shock to move from Quebec to North Vancouver to a log cabin at Anahim Lake with no plumbing in it. Ranching afforded groceries but very few frills.

I cashed in an old insurance policy that had been started for me as a child and bought a property, across Corkscrew Creek from where we lived, from Tommy Holte. The property was in two parcels totalling 160 acres. The price was $1,875, one of the best investments I ever made.

When my kids were very young I had a story for each of them about how I got them. I told Cary, the oldest, that I was in Japan one time and a terrible typhoon started up.

Andrea and Chuck, two of my three children.

When the wind finally died down I heard a voice calling for help and I found her trapped under some wreckage and rescued her and took her home with me, and that was why her nickname was Cary Yoto Moto.

I told Chuck that I was out riding one day when a team of horses hooked to a chuck wagon came thundering by me. They were running as fast as they could and there was no driver. I heard a voice in the back of the wagon hollering for help. I took off after it as fast as my horse could go and pulled a little boy out of the chuck wagon just before it went over a bank. I took him home and called him Chuck, after the chuck wagon.

I told Andrea how she got the nickname "Porky." I was burning the old grass off the meadow one day when I heard a voice calling for help. I discovered her and a porcupine close to the fire. I rescued her and took her home and that was why we called her Porky.

All my kids learned to ride horses at an early age and competed in the local gymkhanas. I'm not sure Chuck always enjoyed riding. One day when I was chasing some ornery cattle with him, I told him that cows must be the dumbest animals on earth. "Oh no," he replied, "they are the second dumbest." I guess that didn't say much for us.

We went fishing and camping every chance we got. Each year we would go to the Okanagan for the swimming. Sometimes we swam in Corkscrew Creek but it was awfully cold. On our way to the Okanagan, we would stop at different points of interest. Wildlife parks were especially interesting. So were circuses if one happened to be around.

To determine who would do the dishes at home, one of us would write down a hidden number between 1 and 100. Whoever guessed the number had to do the dishes. If the guess was too high, the next guess had to be lower. If too low, the next guess had to be higher. The one who wrote down the number had to pick the next higher or lower number. If 62 was picked it would be too low, so the next pick would be between 62 and 100. When it was the writer's turn, he or she had to pick 63. It didn't take many picks before you had

The Anahim Lake Post Office (left) was run by Thelma and Earl McEnroy (who was also the local mechanic). Their house is on the right.

Me, Chuck and Earl McEnroy after a fishing trip on the Atnarko River.

very few choices. Chuck liked doing dishes about as much as most kids like eating cod liver oil. In the dozens of times this game was played, we had all seen him pick the number on the first guess. Hilarious for the girls and me but disgusting for him. He still doesn't like doing dishes.

Every ranch in the Anahim Lake area was headquartered on a creek. The household needed water, livestock needed water and the fields needed water for irrigation. These creeks were great for what we needed, but they could be treacherous for the young children who were raised on them. The creeks flooded every spring when the snow melted. At least one family lost a child to a creek. Stanley Dowling's daughter Patsy fell into the Klinaklini River on their ranch, but caught a cable stretched across the river and was rescued. Stan told me much later that after they rescued her, she had told him she couldn't have drowned because she had hold of the cable. She was very young at the time. Tommy Engebretson fell into the Dean River in front of his parents' house. He was able to latch onto something stretched across the river and was pulled to safety. When Corkscrew Creek was high, it was a silty, muddy, mean-looking body of fast-moving water. When the river went down after spring thaw, the water became crystal clear and the creek itself became beautiful. Its banks were lined with willows, spruce and jackpine.

We often took the kids swimming and fishing in the river during the summer, and all three kids learned to swim in it. From where it ran into Anahim Lake to where it started in Corkscrew Basin, there were fish in it. High up in Corkscrew Basin I have ridden across small trickles of water that run down to Corkscrew Creek, and I have seen small fish in them.

The kids were not allowed to go to the creek without an adult. We stressed the fact that it could be very dangerous, as most of the banks were steep and you wouldn't be able to get out of the river if you got into it. Cary seemed to have a special fascination for playing in the creek. One day I went down to the creek at the crossing by the house and saw her shoes stuck in the mud in the shallow water. She had obviously fallen backwards away from the creek instead of forward into deeper water. I went up to the house and explained to her very seriously that she must never go near the creek

The Anahim Lake Community Hall. One winter during a heavy snowfall, we lit the stove in preparation for a community show. Before anyone was able to attend, the roof collapsed and flattened all the chairs.

Fantastic fishing: me, Judy and Earl McEnroy. Earl and I strung the fish on a pole and packed them out of the Atnarko where we ran into the game warden on the trail. We had the exact legal limit of fish.

alone again. She seemed to understand and I thought the danger was over. About two days later I saw her playing right beside the creek on a steep bank. Had she fallen in there, we wouldn't even have known where she was. This time I broke a little switch off a willow bush and we got to the house in record time. The lesson was learned but neither one of us enjoyed it.

One day I went out to check the fence around one of our pastures and Andrea wanted to come. I was riding a gentle horse we called Argo, so I put her on behind me. As the pasture was on the other side of Corkscrew Creek, I rode up the creek to a crossing. The water was a little high and dirty, but Argo was a tall horse and could easily wade it. We proceeded across the creek without incident until we had almost reached the other side. A small tree leaning away from the bank and under the water got caught between the horse's hind legs. He gave a hell of a lurch to get clear of it, and instantly we lost our passenger. I knew if Andrea went under in that muddy water she would be awfully hard to locate, so I rolled backwards off the horse and got hold of her almost immediately.

A knack with horses (under most circumstances).

With Andrea in tow, I waded out of the creek about the same time Argo did. We rode along that side of the creek, down to the bridge on the main road, and back up to the house. The fence didn't get checked and we had a chilly ride home.

As the kids got older, they went riding on their own. We had several good saddle horses on the ranch. One they liked was called Flash, an all-round good horse, gentle but with lots of life. I had ridden him for years in the mountains and chased cattle and horses with him, and I thought he was foolproof. Chuck complained about Flash running away with him, but Chuck was fairly young at the time and I thought it must be his lack of experience. I was soon to learn something new about Flash. Not long after Chuck complained about him, I was chasing some cattle down the main Morrison Meadow Road with Flash. I had an old hackamore on him. The cattle tried to turn off the main road and go up the road to Andy and Irene Lendvoy's ranch. I ran Flash around the cattle and turned them back onto the main road. But when Flash hit the side road he was down it as fast as he could run. The bosal of the hackamore had slipped up on his nose and I had little control of him. The road was narrow and ditched on either side, so to try and turn him off the road would have been a disaster. I had visions of going through the gate at the end of the road whether it was closed or open, when I noticed Flash was paying attention to a flat piece of ground coming up on the left side of the road. We shot off the road at this point onto some smooth ground, and the runaway was over. Thank goodness. From then on I was much more careful with my hackamore, and I understood how Chuck had got into trouble.

The other saddle horse, Argo, once gave me a different kind of ride. I was riding him way up Christensen Creek, north of Cless Pocket Ranch, hunting deer. By the time I started for home it was getting dark. Between me and the ranch were some huge swamps, with only a narrow passageway of good going through them. As it was so dark I couldn't tell where the trail was, I gave Argo his head and let him choose the way back. Horses have an uncanny way of finding their way in the wilderness. I thought that Argo would just hit the trail we had come up on, two or three miles below us. Instead he took us on a shortcut that led us through the middle of an almost impassable swamp. There were times when I didn't know if he could go on, but there wasn't much I could do but let him try. If I got off and led him in this kind of going, I would get stepped on. If I left him and floundered my way out alone, I would have a problem finding him if he got bogged down. We finally got through the swamp and back on hard ground again and home to the Cless Pocket Ranch. We were a lot muddier than when we left, but I'm not sure we were much wiser.

The crossing at the headwaters of Corkscrew Creek.

When I was ranching on Corkscrew Creek I hired schoolkids to help me put up the hay. By this time we had tractors to help with the work. Alymer Ratcliff, Robby Stewart and my brother-in-law John Brecknock were three of the boys I can remember. The ones that stayed on the ranch slept in a machine shop at one end of a big, long building I had built to keep firewood in. To wake them up early in the morning, I would stand in front of the house and throw rocks at the machine shop. What this must have sounded like inside I can only guess, but I know it was a good alarm clock because nobody ever missed breakfast. John Brecknock became a staff sergeant in the RCMP, Robby Stewart owns and operates a famous fishing lodge on the Dean River, and Alymer builds log buildings in Bella Coola. One young fellow working for us was the son of one of the editors for *Reader's Digest,* and he wrote me a nice letter thanking me for his experiences on the ranch. Maybe these youngsters learned more than just when to get up in the morning.

In my spare time I would work at any decent job I could get. The ranch was great to live on, great for the kids, but the money was damned poor. One of the jobs Judy and I got was running the store in the town of Anahim Lake when my parents went on their annual vacation. It wasn't hard for us to see that the store offered opportunities that a small ranch couldn't possibly give us. We got $300 a month plus board just to run the store. That was real good money at the time.

In 1967 my parents sold the Cless Pocket Ranch to Evan Sleeman, and they decided to retire to Victoria. They offered the store to me for $25,000, no interest and no money down. The payments were $200 a month for a little over ten years. That sounds easy today, but it wasn't. There was little money in the country and we were just able to make our payments.

One thing I started in the store that was probably unique in the retail business was to let the customer flip double or nothing for anything they bought. The odds in flipping are fifty-fifty. In a thousand flips, I should win five hundred times. I would flip one coin and the customer would flip another. One of us would have to

My old store (circa 1969) served the region for years, but when it burned down it was a blessing in disguise—I hadn't realized how outdated it had become until I rebuilt it.

call odd or even, meaning a head and a tail, or two heads or two tails. At first we flipped the coin, then caught it and placed it on the back of the other hand, but too many coins were dropped and shifted, so the coin had to be palmed flat on the counter.

The double or nothing coin flip certainly broke the monotony of selling peanuts and provided me with quite a bit of amusement. To add to the fun, I would always ask the person who flipped with me to please give me my coin back. I would even do this when it was his coin. The coin flip itself was controlled, so it was a hundred percent fair and honest. After the flip, the object of the game was to get an extra coin. Sometimes the flip would get quite exciting, and you would be surprised at how easy it was to forget who had produced the coins. If a customer lost or won, I would usually tell him there were no hard feelings and nothing personal about the flip.

For quite a while one of my extra jobs was to sell gas for airplanes on the airstrip next to the town. One day I flipped a pilot double or nothing for the gas I had just sold him. As we had let our

Paul Lowrie flips double or nothing. The picture shows good flipping technique with our hands flat on the counter.

coins drop on the ground, he not only paid double for his gas, but I was able to get his coin. What I didn't know was the pilot had a passenger who had videotaped the whole scene. I was caught red-handed picking up his coin and had to give it back. Of course I told him there would be no hard feelings.

A fellow from the Nazko area used to flip for his summer trail-ride provisions. I won one year and lost one year. That was the most expensive flip I had done. It came to several hundred dollars, and it was lucky we broke about even.

One day at the end of August in 1977, a young university student working for Ken Pratt down the Dean River for the summer came into the store and fell in love with a tanned fox skin I had for sale that was hanging on a nail behind the counter. His name was Peter Shaughnessy, and he was unusually tall for anyone around Ana-him Lake. He was a basketball player for Simon Fraser University, about six feet, nine inches tall. I could tell he was pretty interested in buying the fox. He asked me how much it was and I told him it was $90, but it might not cost him anything. He brightened up, hearing this. When I told him about the double or nothing deal I extended to all customers, he was quite hesitant. Finally he made up his mind to flip, and I explained how it had to be done. He took a coin, and he must have been crouched down when he flipped it, because I thought he was going to follow the coin to the ceiling before he caught it. In the end the fox cost him $180 and damned near a heart attack. Years later, when I stopped for a coffee at the Tatla Lake café, I noticed a guy looking in my direction. I didn't recognize him, and finally he came over to me and asked if I remembered flipping double or nothing for a fox hide in my store. Of course I hadn't forgotten the flip, as it was the funniest flip I had ever made. He said the fox cost him two months' wages. He said he had made $200 brushing trails for Ken Pratt that summer and only had $20 and the fox fur to show for his summer earnings before heading back to school in Vancouver. I told him it was no wonder he had been so nervous. We had a good laugh before going our separate ways. He said he still had the fox fur, minus the tail. His dog had chewed it off.

Three years after buying the store, I BS'ed the bank out of enough money to buy half interest in the Frontier Inn, the local café, with my sister-in-law, Toni Brecknock. The Frontier Inn was licensed to sell beer with a sandwich, had cabins to rent and was a fairly profitable business.

When I was growing up in Bella Coola, relaxation always seemed to be accompanied by liquor consumption. On Sundays when the store closed, my dad would gather some close friends and organize a fishing trip up the valley, and he would soon become more interested in drinking than fishing. As the saying goes, as monkey sees, monkey does. On the Cless Pocket Ranch we worked long hours, six days a week, and on the seventh day we almost always saw how much booze we could drink. We would ride horses to the town of Anahim Lake and party with anybody who wanted to party. Eventually we got an old car and went into town in style.

After one party I woke up early in the morning in the post office. I had crawled into an empty mail sack for a sleeping bag, and I had no recollection of getting there. Another time a few of us polished off a bunch of cheap wine in the bunkhouse on the ranch, and when I woke up in the morning the place smelled so gross from spilled wine that I could never drink wine again.

I don't remember ever getting sick from drinking. Monday morning was just the start of another working week. The yearly stampede was the only time I ever drank more than one day at a time. After buying the store, that became my busiest time of the year and I just didn't have time to drink when the stampedes were on.

There were a lot of people in the country who seemed to run on whisky. Don Widdis, known as "Squeaky," who drove truck from Williams Lake to Bella Coola, told me one time that a gallon of "vino" flattened the Bella Coola Hill like the prairies. Once we were passing on the road going in different directions and we stopped to chat. The first thing he did was offer me a drink of gin. He said if I didn't like gin I'd had breakfast, lunch and supper. Squeaky was about the norm for a lot of truck drivers in those days.

Running three businesses and relaxing with too much booze wasn't conducive to a stable marriage, and Judy and I parted company in the late 1960s. I wound up single for a few years. We had been together about ten years and our oldest daughter, Cary, was about nine.

Heavy drinking in the developing Chilcotin and neighbouring communities has often been lionized, but there is another side to this fable. There are tales of truck drivers getting out of their trucks after long trips over slow dirt roads, so drunk they could barely walk. On one occasion a local rancher flagged down a tourist on the Chilcotin Highway and asked him for help to find his Cat. The tourist looked all over for a house cat until he finally realized the rancher was looking for a missing bulldozer. Eventually he heard the treads churning in the gravel and found the Cat butted up against a large tree, still running. The rancher was intoxicated and had fallen off the bulldozer while attempting to urinate off it while it was still moving. When he had come to after passing out for a brief period of time, he wandered off following the tracks in the opposite direction. This rancher had once told me that when he was on a drinking spree, he had to have a bottle beside his bed when he retired so he could have a drink whenever he woke up during the night.

Ken Thompson and Lester Dorsey chat it up. Ken smoked almost continually until one day he just up and quit. A remarkable guy.

There were always good people who couldn't handle liquor. A married couple, who are now retired, once had very good jobs. The lady was used to having a few drinks after work, and retirement brought her the opportunity to expand the habit. She was soon drinking in the morning and not stopping until she went to bed, and after a couple of drinks in the morning she ended up in her own little world until she passed out at night. They never took any trips or holidays because of her condition.

Some people get away with heavy drinking and then eventually control it to the point where it doesn't damage their lives. Many others have their lives destroyed by too much booze. Several of my family members have died from drinking over a period of years. Others have had their husbands or wives simply vegetate from steady drinking. Most of the heavy drinkers I have known have had their lives shortened by alcohol. I have seen statistics that link alcohol to twice as many deaths as all illicit drugs combined, and that show the number of people hospitalized from drinking has gone up by 17 percent in the last ten years. That is the other side of the story.

Eventually it was time to get out of ranching. The government had a program that allowed small ranchers to borrow money to improve their holdings. They could buy machinery, break land or even fix up their living quarters. I never backed down from borrowing money if I could visualize a gain down the road. These government-sponsored loans went through the Farm Credit Corporation (now Farm Credit Canada). I bought new equipment, put plumbing in the house and shined the ranch up pretty good, then put it up for sale through a realtor. It wasn't too long before a Texan and his wife arrived with an interest in buying a ranch.

Anything from Texas is supposed to be big. The fellow from Texas, by the name of Corky Williams, had to stretch up in his cowboy boots to reach five feet. He bought my ranch on Corkscrew Creek and he turned out to be quite a character. He found a place he liked better than the one he bought from me, so he sold out and bought a ranch about ten miles farther down the Dean River. Corky introduced the first round baler to the area. Years later, when I

Me, Chuck and Bob Smith. Bob was then married to my sister, Loy. Chuck was visiting from Williams Lake where he worked for the School District.

would fly my plane down the Dean River during haying season, he would jump up on a bale of hay and give me a full moon. Any time I had someone with me I would fly as low and slow as I could so my passengers could get a good view of Corky's performance. This soon became a ritual on these flights. Not too many pilots could offer their passengers that kind of a show. Corky was an actor and cowboy poet and always full of piss and vinegar. He often tried to see how much liquor a small man could hold. I watched him do this several times and never could see how he got better at it.

♠ STANLEY DOWLING

The store I owned had been built by a hard-driving entrepreneur by the name of Stanley Dowling. Stan started his first store in 1937, at Bert Lehman's ranch six miles east of Anahim Lake, and then moved to the present location in downtown Anahim Lake. Before that, groceries and ranching supplies were brought to Anahim Lake by packhorses from Bella Coola. Stanley was the first person to start trucking supplies to Anahim Lake from Vancouver. The road was barely passable when it was good, and after a serious rain or snowfall, it was much worse.

During the war years Stan would be on the so-called road most of the time, and he had a well-known trader, Alf Lagler, run the store for him. This arrangement went on for some eight years until Stan and his wife Edna got out of the store business. In 1943 they bought a ranch at Kleena Kleene. They ranched there for sixteen years, and he and Edna raised four daughters, Margery, Maureen, Marilyn and Patsy. He told me he gave up trying to have a boy and called the last one Pat.

When Stan was younger, before I knew him, he had a reputation for liking his suds. Apparently he liked to drink in beer parlours with his cronies and sometimes got into heated debates. If an argument couldn't be settled verbally at the table, Stan wasn't averse to settling it away from the beer table, and he wasn't an easy man to handle there either.

Gordon Wilson and I had been doing some ranch work when the saddle horse and I both got thirsty. Gordon was standing by and caught the moment on camera. PHOTO GORDON WILSON

When I knew Stan, I was driving the Cless Pocket Ranch truck and Stan was hauling freight for his ranch. Our paths would often cross at Benny Abbott's beer parlour in the Maple Leaf Hotel in Williams Lake. Stan would be telling some funny story and would laugh harder than anyone he was telling it to. One of his jokes was about a priest and a rabbi discussing things they had done during their lives. The rabbi asked the priest if he had ever eaten a ham sandwich. The priest said he had, then asked the rabbi if he had ever tried having sex. The rabbi was kind of shocked by this question and said, "Certainly not." The priest said: "Well you should try it. It's a lot better than a ham sandwich." Stan told me how he once got Gus Jakel to open his beer parlour in the Chilcotin Hotel in Alexis Creek before the legal opening time, and stayed until it closed. He figured he had established some sort of record and I don't doubt that he had.

Stan had the agency for selling Massey Ferguson tractors and attachments. When I was working on the Cless Pocket Ranch I bought a Massey 50 with a mower from him. The unit cost three thousand dollars and I charged three dollars an hour for it. The tractor mower immediately made horse-drawn mowers a thing of the past. Stan sold so much equipment that he called his ranch the Clean-'em Clean Ranch. Alf Lagler died in 1987, and as a tribute to his old friend and helper, Stan wrote the following, which was published in the Williams Lake newspaper.

> *You came into this world*
> *All naked and bare,*
> *You went out of this world*
> *To God knows where,*
> *You were all right here*
> *So you'll be all right there.*

♠ IKE SING

Ike Sing was born in Merritt, BC, and grew up in a family of four boys and four girls. He first came to Anahim Lake on a hunting trip just after the Second World War, and he met Lester and Mickey Dorsey, Thomas Squinas, and Harold and Alice Engebretson.

Ike must have liked the country and his new-found friends, because he returned to Anahim Lake the next fall. He learned that Stan Dowling had bought the McClinchy Ranch at Kleena Kleene and had leased his store to a fellow by the name of Gordon McGinnis.

About the time Ike arrived in 1946, Stan's store burned down. It was easy for Ike's new friends to talk him into opening a store next to the reserve in Anahim Lake. Because Chinese people weren't permitted to hold title to land in the years around the war, Ike put the property in Harold Engebretson's name. About this time my father, Andy Christensen, bought the land in Anahim Lake that Stan Dowling owned. He moved his ranch store to that property and hired Alf Lagler to run it for him. There certainly was no shortage of competition for Ike.

Ike's brother Jimmy worked with him for quite a while when Ike was getting the store up and running. Jimmy was quite a bit younger than Ike and was a jolly guy full of life, but the state of night life in Anahim Lake probably discouraged Jimmy from taking root in the community.

Like all stores in Anahim Lake, Ike's store burned down, and like all stores in Anahim Lake, it was rebuilt. Lou Holtry, who ranched east of Anahim Lake with his wife, Babe, once told me that ranchers were stubborn bastards or they wouldn't be ranchers. I guess it was the same way with store owners. Ike built a new store and eventually put in cabins to rent to people travelling through. He also fed the guests who rented space from him. He was a very good host and an interesting conversationalist.

On his return from one of his trips to Vancouver, Ike brought along an elderly Chinese man by the name of Mr. Ye. Mr. Ye was an excellent cook and was the main cook at Ike's place for a fair stretch of time. He spoke very little English but didn't have to. On meeting him you knew you were in the presence of a very fine

Alf Lagler, Andrew Collins and Andy with grandson Chuck. Alf and Andrew Collins were partners in a store next to the Native reserve for a long time.

D'Arcy, Ike Sing, Harold Engebretson, Chuck Christensen and Rod (one of Tommy Holte's sons) in front of the store.

elderly gentleman. Ike Sing once told a few of us, "You think I can cook, but I don't know nothing compared to Mr. Ye." Ike deserved a little more credit than he gave himself, but Mr. Ye was a fine cook. Where he came from or where he went, none of us ever knew. He just showed up one year, and another year he was gone.

Ike's business did very well with the opening of the Bella Coola Road. It has been said that 90 percent of the success of a business is its location. Ike was certainly in the right location, and he had the personality to go with it. One night when I was talking to him I kidded him about all the money he was making. I expected him to self-consciously deny this and got a kick out of his reply. "Why shouldn't I be well paid?" he said. "I'm a damned smart-looking little guy."

Ike was also a very tenacious person. He told me once that if you couldn't win with a .22 rifle, you would just have to get a 30-30, but you would eventually win. He wasn't referring to shooting anyone,

Harold and Ike: Two old-timers enjoying their twilight years.

of course. He was saying that when you had a goal in mind, you found a way to achieve it.

In 1960, Ike sold his business to Ed Escott, and Ed's daughter, Marilyn, and her husband, Don Baxter, ran it for some thirty years. He retired to a few acres of farmland in Cawston, BC, and married a Chinese lady. He had always had a green thumb, and he grew fruit and vegetables on his new place. When Kris and I stopped in to see him, he told us that he had to spray his fruit by law, and he was sure this made him feel kind of sick.

There was quite a bit of grey matter in the Sing family. Jimmy went on to be an accountant; Ike's nephew, Larry, was a medical doctor; and there were other professionals in the family. Ike and his wife had a son who also became a doctor, and went on to specialize in urology in Toronto. "Not only is he a doctor," Ike lamented, "but he had to be a specialist and now I don't see him no more."

Ike has since passed on. My friends Donald and Terry Egan went to the service for Ike. They were welcomed by the relatives and friends in attendance and practically treated like part of the family. They returned home with even more fond memories of Ike.

WINNING AT POKER
& STAMPEDE

I'M NOT SURE WHEN I STARTED PLAYING POKER, BUT IT WAS probably on the Cless Pocket Ranch, during summer holidays when I was still in school. I played with one of the hired hands for whatever odds and ends I could dig out of my pockets—string, matches, the odd coin. I could see the fellow I was playing against was a real good player as he drew three kings every time he dealt. We were playing in the ranch workshop one day when Billy Dagg, the ranch foreman and my mentor, came into the room. I told Billy how good the ranch hand was and how he got three kings half the time he played. Billy broke up the game and made the fellow give back anything he had won from me.

For some of the crew, a poker game seemed to break out during every spare moment on the ranch. We used washers for chips, three sizes of them to serve as nickels, dimes and quarters. Ollie Nukalow, a big, strong mixed-blood (his other name was Johnny Robertson), and I would go partners and at the end of the game we would split what we had won. Ollie's half-brother, Scotty Gregg, always called me his brother's partner. The partnership won more than it lost, so it seemed like a good arrangement, even though very little real money changed hands. Money was scarce in those days—we earned wages of three to five dollars a day. I always paid close attention to the game and learned a lot.

Poker used to be played with cash. Now it is almost always played with
chips as this is both faster and an easier way to keep track of money.
I'm looking at the camera and Doug Norberg is on the right.

When I went back to school in the fall, I played poker with my
own age group and also with some of the older players in Bella
Coola. The local policeman, Ernie Bradley, and some of my uncles
and whoever else showed up would quite often have a game. The
year I finished high school I had $1,000 in the bank from poker.
That was a good chunk of money in 1948.

Over the years I had some especially memorable games of
poker. When I was working on the Cless Pocket Ranch, a Russian fellow by the name of Ivan Demininico stopped by. He had
barely escaped from Communist Russia, made his way to Canada
and somehow got to Anahim Lake and wanted to go back in the
bush to live. I noticed that he often used the word *bastard* in his
broken English, whether it made sense or not. He finally said he
wanted to play poker, which was all right with me. It wasn't long
before the game was going heavily in my favour. Then he finally

made a fairly large bet. It was pretty evident he had a good hand. Before I could throw my hand away, he reached over to my money and called himself. Then he said, "Well, I win, bastard." That was the only time I had someone bet me in a poker game and then call himself with my money. I thought it was funny and just let him take the pot.

Before Ivan left the ranch, he bought a horse from me. He picked the one he wanted and I roped it in a corral full of horses and gave him the rope. Something else came up and I had to leave him with the horses. While I was gone he tied the loose end of the lariat to the fence and let the other horses out the gate. Of course the horse he had tied up thought it was free too, until it hit the end of the rope. When Ivan finally caught up with me, he said, "Horse bastard run away and broke its neck bastard." I had never thought anyone would do something like that, but I guess I should have known better. I gave him a deal on another horse and the last I saw of him, he was heading out for the Blackwater country.

Another memorable poker opponent was an American by the name of Bob Anthony. He and his wife, Dorothea, had bought the Home Ranch from Pan Phillips, a lifetime friend of my family. They wanted to make the ranch into a working cattle and guest ranch. Several cabins were built and Bob hauled a big one-way disc in his plane from Anahim Lake, to break up more land for hay production. Bob came into the store quite often when he was in Anahim Lake and I got to know him pretty well.

One day Bob came in just as I was closing. He got what he needed and as the sun was over the yardarm, as the saying goes, I proposed an evening drink. This seemed to be a good idea, so we settled down to BS'ing over a few drinks, and somehow we decided to play poker. Normally I didn't drink while playing poker, but this was more of a social event than a poker game. The game and drinks went along well and we were commencing to have a real good evening. Eventually I got a run of good cards and Bob ran out of cash, so he started writing IOUs on small pieces of paper he found in the office. I had quite a few IOUs when it was decided I had better

My cousin Aubrey. Part of his ranch was on Anahim Lake and part was ten miles to the east of Lilly Lake. PHOTO ELEANOR CHRISTENSEN.

mix us a couple of drinks. When I got back with the drinks and sat down to continue the poker game, I thought the stack of IOUs had gone down considerably, but we weren't playing for very big stakes so I didn't worry about it. But the next time I went to replenish our drinks I kept better track of the table we were playing on, and this time I found out where the IOUs were going. Bob grabbed a few IOUs and stuck them in his mouth and ate them. When I returned to the table with the drinks, I asked him what the hell he thought he was doing. He said he was hungry, and as I didn't have any-thing to eat lying around, he thought he'd snack on the IOUs. I told him we would finish the bottle and I would get some supper made before he got indigestion from the IOUs. I also told him to forget about the IOUs he had eaten—I wasn't going to follow him around to try and retrieve them. It had been an interesting evening.

While I was still going to school in Bella Coola, I had a game of poker with my cousin Aubrey Christensen and Tommy Holte,

Tommy Holte dressed for minus sixty degree (F) weather: a hat with ear flaps, leather mitts with wool liners and the mandatory long johns. His Cowboy King denim jacket is layered over a wool pullover and another heavy shirt, and his Cowboy King denim jeans are covered by leather chaps. Inside his rubber boots are felt insoles, plus two pair of wool socks. Felt liners would come later on.

my dad's right-hand man on the ranch. Tommy and his family were some of the earliest non-Native settlers in the area. Tommy's brother Jimmy was the grandfather of Carey Price, the famous hockey player from Anahim Lake who went on to play for the Montreal Canadiens. Aubrey and I were planning to set out on a three-day horseback ride to the valley the next morning. All of us would have had a few bucks from haying all summer, and as it turned out Aubrey and I wound up adding a little to our summer stakes. As we were leaving the table after the game, Tommy looked at us and said, "Chrish" — his way of saying "Christ"

An older Tommy (circa 1989) dressed for summer.

— "I don't mind losing a few dollars to you guys, but you'll probably take that money to Bella Coola and piss it agin' the wall." Tommy was a great guy and a hell of a hard worker. I remember chasing cattle with him one time when his saddle horse wasn't working as well as it should. Instead of getting mad at the horse, as many riders would have, he turned to me and said, "Chrish, he tries the best he can anyway."

Nobody wins every time they play poker. I always figured if you could win 70 percent of the time, you would be pretty lucky. This would mean you would lose 30 percent of the time. Sometimes your losses are larger than your winnings, so you are still walking a fine line. I always had a good understanding of math. Pot odds and the odds of catching a hand I was drawing to came natural at an early age. A lot of players would draw to hands that I wouldn't even consider drawing to. Luck is a big factor in any poker game.

One time on the Cless Pocket Ranch I got into a game with my grandfather, Adolph, my cousin Aubrey and some other players. I got a horrible run of cards and lost the equivalent of a month's wages. This was the worst loss I had ever had up to that time, and I literally felt sick. I didn't realize at the time that it was one of my great learning experiences in poker. You never bellyache or complain. You suffer in silence and learn from your losses. You are supposed to win like you're used to winning, and lose like you like losing.

Recently I had a four-month run of losing poker. I didn't come close to winning a tournament and won very seldom in a cash game. The odds against a losing streak like this must be millions to one, but you go through dozens of dealers and countless different decks of cards on many different tables, and terrible hands seem to follow you everywhere. I'm glad the stakes weren't high and that I have learned to play tighter than a knat's ass stretched over Mount Everest. You also learn in poker never to play for more than you can afford to lose. Going into a game without enough money is like hunting a grizzly bear with a switch.

Dolly Parton and the Queen wound up at the Pearly Gates together. Saint Peter said he only had room for one, and the other would have to wait. He asked each one to show him why she should go first. Dolly bared her ample breasts and told him they were the best pair in the whole world. The Queen peed in a toilet and flushed it. Saint Peter immediately let her into heaven first. "Dolly," Saint Peter said, "you should know a royal flush always beats a pair."

One thing besides death, taxes and poker that always happened in Anahim Lake was the annual stampede. People came from all over the country to have a good time and visit with friends they hadn't seen for a long time, or at least since the last stampede. The first stampedes in the area took place in the Bella Coola Valley from 1931 to 1936. They were called the Stuie Stampedes and were held up on the little flat just north of Stuie Lodge, four or five miles from the end of the road from Bella Coola to Anahim Lake. The lodge had been built by A.J. Arnold and Tommy Walker.

In 1937 the stampede was held at Bert Lehman's ranch, a few miles east of Anahim Lake. Those early stampedes had no fences or chutes. For a rider to mount a bucking horse, the animal had

L to R: Uncle Helmer and his retriever, Fred Cameron (an insurance sales-man) and Billy Dagg. These men were good shots, but they also had the advantage of an abundance of targets.

to be blindfolded. Once the rider got on, the horse was let loose to buck in an open area not contained by a fence. It took one hell of a good pickup man to handle this situation. Billy Dagg, a noted horseman, was the first one.

Stan Dowling had his first store on Bert Lehman's ranch and he pushed hard for the 1937 stampede. In 1938 he built a new store in Anahim Lake and cut about ten miles of road to hook the main road to his store, so the road from Williams Lake no longer went through Bert Lehman's. Throughout the war years, Dowling ran the stampede in the town of Anahim Lake. A proper arena with chutes for livestock and a fenced-in bucking area had now been built. During the war years liquor was rationed, but rations must have been saved for the Anahim Lake Stampedes because they were not noted as sobriety contests. The dances were held in a garage Stan had built near his store. For a while the music was supplied by Michel Moffat, a local Native. He played the accordion and I think he only knew one piece of music, called the Ulka-tcho two-step or stomp—well suited for a lubricated garageful of

L to R: Jimmy Holte's wife Teresa with her baby; Johnny Web, Jimmy Holte on the guitar and Howard Harris on banjo.

dancers. I believe Michel had the only one-man band in history that could keep everybody dancing for four nights in a row with one song. For two weeks after the stampede, you could still hear the music.

As the years passed, the stampede got bigger. The local Cattlemen's Association started running it, and all labour that went into the stampede was voluntary. The Cless Pocket Ranch, then owned by my dad, supplied the cattle needed for riding, milking, roping and the rest. Brahma bulls were still unheard of. The music was now supplied by Howard Harris from Quesnel on banjo, and locals Earl McInroy, banjo; his wife, Thelma, on accordion; her sister, Lorena Draney, piano; the two ladies' brother, Harold Engebretson, violin; and Jimmy Holte on guitar and vocals. These six musicians could get a crowd jumping pretty high. Harold told me that one night a guy came up to the stand and asked them to play a different beat, and Howard Harris told the guy the only beat he would get was right over the head. "So you see," Harold said, "this music business can even get dangerous."

Money was very scarce, and even with all volunteer labour the Cattlemen's Association had trouble balancing the books. In the early 1960s, as they didn't have any cash in the bank to start the stampedes, they put out a feeler at their spring meeting to see if anybody had a solution. Pan Phillips and I were at the meeting and we had both long ago learned to be careful with the dollar to survive. It had been said that between the two of us, we would have no trouble squeezing a nickel until the beaver shit. We came up with an idea for running the concession stand. We would put up $250 cash per year for five years, and in return we would get the concession rights on the stampede grounds. This arrangement was to turn out well for all parties involved.

In getting the concession stand ready for our first day on the job at the Anahim Lake Stampede, Pan and I had to find a cool place to put the wieners and hamburger patties, as there was no refrigeration on the grounds. We dug a hole at the back of the concession

L to R: George Pennoyer, me in the foreground, Alan Styvesant (one of the Frontier Cattle Company's financial backers) and Pan.

stand and it looked like it would work perfectly. When we got our supplies the next day, we would put the meat in the hole and put a simple lid over it and we'd be on our way. On arriving the next morning we discovered that during the night, someone had used our refrigerator for a toilet. Fortunately it didn't take us long to figure out how to fix a fridge in those days. A few shovelfuls of gravel and we were in business. I don't think they had health inspectors in those days.

Pan made a couple of innovations to cut the cost of a cup of coffee. As coffee was cheaper than canned milk, we only punched one hole in the milk can and we filled the cup with coffee as full as we could so there was little room for cream anyway. One day we were shoving out hamburgers as quick as we could when Ronnie Schooner, a huge guy from Bella Coola, came up and bought one. Ronnie was not only a large man, he also had a big sense of humour. He went away with his burger but before long he came back with the pattie in the middle of his hand. In that hand the pattie looked about as big as a fifty-cent piece. He very shortly got a hamburger more to his liking.

Pan and I ran the concession stand for five stampedes. By then the Cattlemen's Association was on firmer footing and took over the concession, and Pan and I were no longer financially involved. I had bought the store in 1967 and the stampedes had given the store business a big boost. The stampedes continued to get bigger and bigger over those years. Tents and campers were crowded right up the Dean River from the stampede grounds, and anyone who got tired of watching the events could go fishing. In four days of stampede we would do as much business in the store as we would do in one of our slack months. We did so well that we started donating money to the event—five hundred dollars a year.

♠ PAN PHILLIPS

I met Pan Phillips when I was a young child. He had been made famous by three books, *Grass Beyond the Mountains, Nothing Too Good for a Cowboy* and *The Rancher Takes a Wife,* all by Rich

Pan was always happy to have his picture taken. Here he is raking hay at his fishing lodge on Tizzy Lake.

Hobson, Jr. Rich was the son of Admiral Richmond P. Hobson, an American war hero who had sunk his ship in the mouth of a harbour in the States, bottling up the Spanish fleet the Americans were fighting at the time. He became such a celebrity that the women at all the high-toned balls he had to go to would run up to meet him and kiss him. According to one story about him in *Reader's Digest*, he got the title of the most kissed man in America.

Pan and Rich drove to Anahim Lake in the fall of 1934 in an old Model A Ford. They built a small cabin two miles up the Dean River from Anahim Lake. The plan was to stay the winter there and go around the Ilgachuz Mountains in the spring and start ranching in the Blackwater country in a big way. Pan had the outdoor savvy and Rich had the enthusiasm and financial backing.

As news of their arrival spread, Cyrus Bryant paid them a visit. He saw right away that they would never make the winter in the cabin they had built. As he said to Alfred, it was so poorly built that you could throw a cat out between the logs. Alfred and Cyrus had been helped a lot when they came to the country, so they took a packhorse and a couple of saddle horses over to Pan and Rich's and talked them into moving to Corkscrew to spend the winter with them.

Road trip with Pan. We are on our way to see Wes Carter and family for a little holiday.

Rich and Pan started the Frontier Cattle Company, later made famous by the books. Rich's big money contacts in the States made it possible at the start, but before he got things rolling, the Second World War broke out and money was no longer available.

Years later, during one of his stopovers on the Cless Pocket Ranch, I wound up in a rowboat with Rich, on a goose hunt. The rest of the party was walking overland from the ranch to the same destination. Rich saw a bare-looking patch up in the Rainbow Mountains about twenty miles away, and started waving his arms and telling me what a big meadow it must be. I was only nine years old but even at my age I knew it was no meadow. Ten years later he and his wife Gloria and my parents celebrated his book *Grass Beyond the Mountains*. The consumption of booze by the visitors was stupendous.

Pan had a great outlook on life. He was enthusiastic about whatever he was doing, even if it was drinking a bottle of whisky. His way of living was catching and I always felt good in his company.

Pan was very superstitious. He told me that once he was out hunting and was fingering the loose shells in his pocket as he rode along. Suddenly he realized that he had thirteen shells. He quickly pulled one out of his pocket and threw it away. Feeling much more relaxed farther on, he rolled a cigarette. When he went to light it he discovered he had thrown his bullet lighter away. Pan built his fishing cabins on some old Native campgrounds, and he told me that some nights he could hear the Indians pounding stakes into the ground. One morning I noticed he had missed a lot of spots while shaving. When I remarked on this, he said he never looked in a mirror. I did not ask why, but I presumed it was something to do with superstition.

Pan Phillips helps us brand some of the cattle we purchased for the C2 Ranch. Wes Carter on the right.

After Pan and I had finished our five-year concession contract with the local stampede committee, Pan started a fly-in fishing camp on Tsetzi Lake in the Blackwater. He got Floyd Vaughan and Johnny Blackwell to build an airstrip on his property in about 1970, and when I began to fly, I used to visit Pan's place often in the summer. I met many of his customers and I was amazed at the way they looked after Pan. They would bring in all the food and drinks they required, which they would share with him. Anything left over when they departed would be left for him. He supplied boats and a roof over their heads and they treated him royally and paid him at the end of their stay. With outside toilets and plain cabins and cookhouse, customers knew they were roughing it in the wild and would never even think of going anywhere else. That was Pan's magnetic effect on a lot of people.

♠ HONEST ED WILLSON

Ed Willson, a guy from Bella Coola, would often stop at the store on his way to or from Williams Lake and Bella Coola. We would have a drink or two and BS a bit. Ed had a contract for getting hydro poles into Bella Coola. On one trip he had to bring in a big machine from

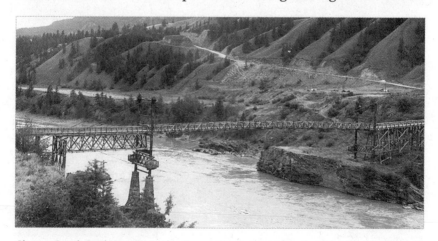

Sheep Creek Bridge, across the Fraser River, tipped so badly with Ed Wilson's big logging machine that he attempted to jump into the river but couldn't get the door open. He was lucky to make it across. COURTESY SAGE BIRCHWATER.

My brother-in-law Jack Ward, Andy Christensen, Ed Collet, me and Bob
Draney taking a break from haying.

Williams Lake, across the old Sheep Creek Bridge over the Fraser
River. He later told me that the old cable bridge tipped so badly that
he had tried to open the door on the machine, with the intention of
jumping. The machine was too wide to get the door open, so he rode
it the rest of the way and made it across safely.

Ed had a lot of get-up-and-go, and he wasn't afraid to try anything. For a while he fished commercially out of Bella Coola, and
he opened a clothing store on the townsite. He called the store
Honest Ed's.

My brother-in-law, Jack Ward, worked on the Cless Pocket
Ranch for a number of years. One day off work, he and I and his
son Pat decided to drive to Bella Coola. There was a lot to see that
was different from the Anahim Lake area. I hadn't been down the
valley for several years and enjoyed it as much as Jack and his son.
We drove as far as the ocean, which is always interesting to see.
On the way back we stopped at Honest Ed's to see Ed Willson. We
exchanged a few pleasantries and then Ed brought out a bottle of
rye whisky. The rye hit the spot quickly, as we hadn't stopped for
lunch. Not long after Ed and I got down to some serious drinking, he produced a deck of cards and we got into a poker game.

The more we drank the wilder the game got. We finished whatever was in the rye bottle, and then we replenished our supply at the Bella Coola liquor store, across the street and a hundred feet or so down the road from Honest Ed's. I don't remember how long we played but we probably started spilling more booze than we were drinking, and the game got right out of hand. Jack must have poured me into our vehicle and headed for Anahim Lake, and I must have slept most of the way back.

The next morning I got up and tried to remember how the poker game had gone. I emptied my pockets and discovered a handful of IOUs made out to me, from Ed. One IOU was written on a letter addressed to Ed's mother that hadn't been opened yet. I mailed the letter back to Ed, along with the other IOUs. In due course I was fully paid all the money owing from that poker game. I guess that is why the store was called Honest Ed's.

♠ SLIM BRECKNOCK

Slim Brecknock, my former brother-in-law, was the announcer for the Anahim Lake Stampede for years. To be a good announcer you need the ability to talk almost continually. Slim was well suited for the job that way, and he seemed to know every contestant at the rodeo and most of the non-contestants. When the song "I Warm So Easy So Dance Me Loose" came out, he adopted it as his theme song. Every once in a while in slack time or between events, he would sing the title to the song. I never did inquire whether he knew any of the other words. Once Slim saw Tommy Engebretson in the crowd watching the stampede and asked him how he liked all the girls that were there. Tommy yelled back that he sure liked the "gooder" ones. This gave Slim another funny opener for his announcing. He always kept the show moving along and he seemed to be enjoying himself thoroughly.

♠ ED ADAMS

While Pan still had his ranch, a fellow by the name of Ed Adams walked into the ranch one morning. He had flown into a nearby lake from Quesnel. The pilot had landed on the wrong side of the lake, causing Ed to stay the night in the bush. He told Pan he had read a lot about him and his way of life, and as he was retired, he offered to work on the ranch without pay, just to be there. I know Pan would have been interested in a deal like that, and I guess a deal was struck.

Ed had been a dairyman in the state of New York, with his parents. He had only missed one milking in thirty years when he got drunk at a horse race. He said he drank a bottle of brandy every day. Being a hell of a hard worker, I guess he burned off the booze during his long workdays. When his parents died he sold the dairy farm, and in his travels he learned of Pan. Having no family of his own, Ed stayed with Pan and his wife, Betty, and their children Diana and Rob. He soon became a hard-working member of the family. Ed was a soft-spoken, well-mannered gentleman. The closest I ever heard him come to swearing when something went wrong was, "Well, mercy." This became his saying, and we flyers used it constantly at Pan's whenever we could fit it in, especially in poker games. Ed worked for Pan on the ranch from 1960 until the ranch was sold in 1969. He had invested his dairy money wisely and had acquired a little place of his own in the Blackwater.

I was flying Ed to Quesnel in the twilight years of his life when he asked me what I thought he should do with the considerable amount of money he had. I suggested he put it into a scholarship fund for students in Quesnel. I don't know how it turned out. One thing for sure, Ed was a well-respected gentleman. Only Pan could have had a hard-working person like Ed come and work for nine years for no money. For this, Ed had found a family he could call his own and an environment that perfectly suited his gentle disposition.

This was probably the best single day of fur buying I had in the Anahim Lake area. The fur hanging on the wings of the plane are probably worth as much as the airplane itself.

OUT OF DEBT
& UP IN THE AIR

OVER THE YEARS IN THE STORE I WAS ALWAYS ABLE TO HIRE GOOD
help. This left me free to pursue other interests from time to time.
One of those interests was real estate. I would find small properties that seemed like good buys and usually did well with them.
Another interest was flying.

I had always wanted to fly a plane, and in 1970 I decided to take
some time off to take lessons. I went to Williams Lake and got Slim
Shirk for an instructor. Slim was a great fellow, a mechanic as well
as an instructor. I think he told me he had twenty thousand hours
of flying under his belt. I'm sure he had that many stories.

Slim gave me the lessons in a Cessna 150, a plane that has a
nose wheel and is very easy to taxi on the strip. It steers much like
a car until you get enough speed for the rudder to take over. With
the nose wheel in front of the plane, the tail is well off the ground,
so forward visibility is excellent. In due course I got my private pilot's licence without difficulty.

When I got back to Anahim Lake, I heard a fellow by the name
of Bill Nickerson had a used Super Cub for sale. As I wanted a
plane for delivering groceries from the store to outlying areas, and
for picking up fur from trappers out in the bush, this was the per-
fect plane for me. The Super Cub has a 150-horsepower Lycoming
engine, and is noted as probably the best two-seater bush plane
ever built. I had recently been in a poker game in Williams Lake

Ronnie Cassam and me gathering fur in Blackwater country with one of my favourite planes, the Bellanca Scout. The skis were bright red.

that had leaned heavily in my favour and won $5,500, the asking price for the plane.

I got someone to fly me down to a little strip near Nickerson's property at Twist Lake, near the foot of Mount Waddington, and looked the plane over. I liked what I saw and a deal was made. The Super Cub has the wheel in the tail and is called a tail-dragger, entirely different from the Cessna 150 I had learned to fly in. Instead of a steering yoke, it had a stick coming out of the floor for directional control. Sitting in a 150, you look down the strip you are going to take off on, much like looking out of a car at the road you are going to drive on. When I got into the Super Cub, the first thing I noticed was I saw a lot more sky than airstrip.

I started the engine. It was already warm from my inspection. I made sure the plane was pointing at the other end of the strip, and gave it full power once it started rolling forward. There was

The Scouts handled beautifully on wheels or skis.

nothing to it. When you point a Super Cub in the right direction and give it full power, you very soon get airborne. The next thing I knew, I was heading back to the strip at Anahim Lake. I accustomed myself to the controls by doing a little banking and turning. I was feeling real good about owning my first airplane.

As I approached the Anahim Lake airstrip I had about forty-five hours of total flying time in a nose wheel or "tricycle-wheeled" plane, and had never landed a tail-dragger before. I came in for a straight-in landing approach, and slowed the plane down. When the wheels touched the strip I pulled off the power, and of course the tail dropped and I was in the unfamiliar position of not being able to see what I was landing on. I immediately applied full power, and when the tail came up I could once again tell what was going on. It took me two more go-rounds before I finally got the beast on the ground, knowing I had some landing problems to iron

D'ARCY CHRISTENSEN

THE FLYING FUR BUYER

Phone 742-3266

BOX 3449
ANAHIM LAKE, B.C.
VOL 1C0

My business card.

out. Slim Shirk had told me that no one he knew had ever starved to death in the air after takeoff. I gave this some serious thought.

After that I went out to the strip almost daily to practise take-offs and landings. These are called touch-and-go's. I was holding down about one in three on the strip. Any of the local gentry who had time to spare would come down and watch my performances. Louise and Cam Moxon, who handled the gas on the strip, were usually among the onlookers, either to cheer me on or to pick up the pieces. I knew one thing—I couldn't keep depending on my for-giving little Super Cub to get me out of trouble in my bad attempts of landing.

When you're playing poker and you get into a tough situation as to what your next move will be, it is said you "go into the tank" to think it out. With this in mind I "went into the tank" on my touch-and-go's. It was obvious that I couldn't control the plane when I touched down on the strip, so I decided to just taxi back and forth on the strip until I had full control of the plane on the ground. In about an hour my landings became much more tolerable and I lost my audience.

The summer of 1970 I bought the Super Cub and delivered groceries to anywhere in the region that had an airstrip, and I got as much enjoyment and flying and landing practice as I could. When winter finally set in, I bought skis for the plane. With skis the whole country became accessible in winter. I could now deliver groceries and pick up furs from all the trappers, both Natives and whites, living in the bush. I was in contact with them on a steady basis. I was flying all the time, buying fur and receiving orders for groceries to be delivered. All someone had to do to get me to land was wave a mink skin at me. I had a very interesting and booming business going.

The only drawback to the metal skis was that when I landed in the snow at certain temperatures, the snow would melt on the bottom of the skis when I was taxiing and then freeze when the plane came to a halt. In order to take off again I had to get the

Johnny and Mary Lou Blackwell receive a load of groceries from my Citabria at their fishing camp on Moose Lake, a business that required a lot of elbow grease. Before Johnny built a landing strip, Floyd Vaughn and I landed in this nearby meadow.

frozen snow off the bottom of the skis. Sometimes I would snow-shoe a good path in front of the plane. Eventually metal skis were replaced by a material that snow would not freeze to, and half the hard work of winter flying was over.

♠

Bush flying wasn't all fun and prosperity, especially in winter. One thing I was always leery of was landing on bad ice. If you went through the ice out in the wilderness, you could be there to stay. I made a rule that I wouldn't land on a lake or river that didn't have caribou or moose tracks on it. Moose and caribou were plentiful, and their tracks were clearly visible from the air.

On one occasion I flew Danny Sill and Edward Leon, two lo-cal Native trappers, out to a lake thirty or so miles northwest of Anahim Lake. I was to drop them off with their supplies so they could trap in the area until spring. The caribou tracks were plenti-ful where I was to land, and the landing was routine. I unloaded my two passengers and their supplies, wished them luck in their trapping, got back in the plane and headed for takeoff. I applied full power but the damned metal skis were sticking badly, and as I slowly gained speed I ran out of caribou tracks. This was the point of no return. It would have been more dangerous to turn around and go back for another run than to keep going forward. The plane finally gained enough speed to get off the ice and just after I was airborne I passed over two huge areas of open water. I was relieved, to say the least.

Another time I had a trapper in a small pothole. It was close to spring and there had been some thawing. The pothole was sur-rounded by trees and I didn't have a lot of room to spare on takeoff. On my first takeoff attempt I could see I wasn't going to make it. I cut the power and used full rudder to slide the plane to a stop. The skis picked up some melted snow near the edge of the pothole and shot a curtain of water outside my window. For a second I thought I had broken through the ice. My second attempt on the track I had broken worked much better. Once again—relief.

Another late winter trip I made was for Marvin Paul on Tsacha

Lake. He had sent a radio message saying he needed groceries. I got a message back to him by phoning the radio station in Quesnel, which sent messages a few times a day to people in isolated areas. I told him to be sure and mark the ice as it was getting close to spring. When the time came for our rendezvous, he had tramped "GOODIES, GOODIES" in the snow on top of the ice. That is one landing I made with confidence.

Another time Mack Squinas and some other trappers sent me a message from Qualcho Lake, down the Dean River from Anahim Lake, for a load of supplies. They told me not to worry about the ice, as they would be there to meet me. I delivered their supplies but I liked Marvin Paul's message a lot better.

When you fly a plane like a Super Cub for two or three hours a day, winter after winter, you get to know almost exactly what you can land on or take off on. Most of the time I was flying in and out of marginal places like potholes and frozen creeks. One day I received word that Larry Smith, my brother-in-law's brother, and his partner, Caroline Bryant, wanted to see me. They lived on a little place west of Nazko. Soon after receiving this information I was flying near where they lived, so I flew over to take a look. I saw immediately that it was going to be very tight. I circled it a couple of times to eye it up real good. If you have to circle three times, my advice is don't land. I had a good approach that went to a small creek and then to a short run of tramped snow. This led to a patch of deep, unmarked snow that had a buck fence on the far side of it that was bordered by tall timber. I came in as low and slow as I could, and when I was sure I would clear the creek, I shut the engine off. I didn't even want the prop idling. When I landed on the packed snow, it was horribly slick. I'm sure I gained speed, and I hit the deep snow going much too fast toward the fence—so fast that when I gave the plane full rudder the plane swung around in a 150-degree arc. I had come very close to giving Larry a fence-repair job. He came down to meet me and we went back to the cabin for coffee and a visit. When I got back to the plane, it wasn't pointed in quite the right direction for takeoff, and it was in a lot of deep snow. With my snowshoes I packed down the snow that I would have to travel over to take off.

Small planes have a handhold welded on the frame of the tail. You use it to lift the tail and turn the plane in the direction you want for takeoff. This is easy to do on ice or when you are flying with wheels, but in deep snow the plane becomes terribly hard to move. Larry was on the plus side of six feet tall and probably over two hundred pounds. I was going to help him turn the plane by kicking the front of the skis as he put pressure on the tail with the handhold. The next thing I knew, he had grabbed the handhold and packed the tail around like the plane was a Tinkertoy. No effort at all. Had the skis stuck, he would have twisted the axles off. But takeoff was easy, and on the way back home I couldn't help but wonder what kind of athlete Larry would have made with the proper training.

When you fly in and out of very marginal places, you also have to be extremely careful not to misjudge wind conditions, length of the landing space, slope of the ground, the possibility of shooting a go-around on trying to land, and so on. One misjudgement can be tolerable, two you very seldom get away with, three can be fatal. In landing at Larry's place, I didn't know how slick my short landing space was. If I had picked up any sort of unnoticed tailwind, or if the deep snow had been less deep or crusted, I would have been in serious trouble.

Three years ago a pilot on floats took off from a remote lake, in a plane fully loaded with passengers and gear. He should have taxied out to where he could take off into the wind, but instead he took off in a crosswind, and home was in the direction the wind was blowing, so he turned downwind. As soon as he did that, he lost the speed of the wind and crashed. Three or four of the passengers never made it out of the plane.

A NOTAM (short for Notice to Airmen) is sent to flyers or people who own airplanes to give them the latest information on anything to do with planes. I received a NOTAM one day stating that alcohol put in the gas tank to get rid of water in the gas

Out of gas. This resulted in two uncomfortable nights outdoors with a fire that kept melting deep into the snow.

might harm the seal in the sediment bowl. I was always careful to strain the gas I used through a special strainer, because sometimes the gas came from barrels. I decided not to use alcohol until I had found out more about it.

On my return trip from visiting Antoine Baptiste, a Native trapper who lived northeast of Anahim Lake, I noticed the gas gauge indicated less gas than it should. When I got to the top of the pass over the Ilgachuz Mountains, there was so little fuel that I had to make an emergency landing. It was late in the afternoon, so I got a fire going and prepared to spend the night. I always had emergency supplies with me and had left an itinerary at the store with my flight plans. I expected one of the other flyers in the area to pick me up in the morning.

But no one came in the morning. Apparently somebody reported seeing me flying down the Dean River, but that had been a day or two earlier, which threw off the calculation of my whereabouts. By the start of the second night my fire had melted to the bottom of four or five feet of snow, and my living quarters remained full of smoke. I should have cut several green logs and built my fire on top of them. This could have kept the fire on top of the snow. Trying to stay warm and sleep under these conditions was very difficult. The side of me that wasn't turned toward the fire would quickly become very cold, and I would have to switch around. Once I dozed off and burned a big hole in my coat. I had plenty of snow to put out the fire in my smouldering coat. My daughter Andrea later told me that people in Anahim Lake came by and sympathized with her over me being missing, but she told them that she knew I was all right and would be found okay.

After two nights in my smoky igloo, I was doubtful that anyone back at the store had read my flight itinerary, and I was seriously considering snowshoeing out. That would have been one hell of a trip. The snow was deep and soft, and I was farther into the mountains than I had thought. Later I took a good look at the route I would have had to take and figured it would have taken three days.

I piled up a bunch of green branches to use for a smoke signal if I heard a plane approaching, but I soon figured out that by the time I got smoke going, any plane searching for me would have passed. From this experience I learned that a searcher ought to keep a sharp look behind, or circle once in a while, looking for this kind of delayed signal.

Around the time I thought again about snowshoeing home, Floyd Vaughan flew over me in his 180, and signalled that he saw me. He flew back to Anahim and sent Wayne Escott in with a Super Cub. I got some gas from him and was glad to see the last of that little camp. Later I figured out that when I had shut the plane off at Antoine's, there was water in the sediment bowl, and it froze and expanded enough that the gas leaked out of the top of the bowl.

One time Floyd was flying a Beaver into Fenton Lake and he got weathered in for the night. The plane was one of Wilderness Airlines' planes from Bella Coola that Dan Schuetze had been flying. When you're flying in the bush, some common advice is to carry a book or two to amuse yourself with while waiting to be rescued. When Floyd got the emergency pack out, all he could find were a few *Playboy* magazines. I forgot to ask him if he had sweet dreams on an empty stomach.

Pat Sill snags a spring salmon in Takia Creek near Tanya Lakes. His son
Gabriel and Lashaway Cahoose stand by ready to assist. PHOTO SAGE BIRCHWATER.

I met Pat Sill and his wife, Minnie, and their family camped
north of Qualcho Lake one winter morning for a prearranged gro-
cery delivery and fur-buying rendezvous. They were camped not
far from the slopes of the Rainbow Mountains, where they were
trapping marten. They had a couple of tents set up and had obviously shovelled the snow out of the way before pitching the tents.
They had a nice fire going to cook on and make coffee. Both tents
faced the fire so they could absorb as much heat as possible. They
were sheltered from the wind by a thick growth of trees behind
them. It was a cozy arrangement with all the comforts of home
in the middle of the vast wilderness. We quickly made a deal on
the marten they had caught and we unloaded the groceries I had
brought. One of their daughters was to fly back to Anahim Lake
with me, so she got settled in the back seat of the plane and we said
farewell to the campers.

I noticed when I prepared to take off that the east end of Qualcho Lake was getting a little obscured from a snowstorm that was forming. It was getting close to spring, and storms were common at that time of year. When I got to the east end of Qualcho Lake, the snow was coming down heavier than I like and visibility was getting very poor. I knew the country I had to fly over very well. I had a compass for direction and took off just over the trees into the falling snow.

My flying instructor, Slim Shirk, once told me that if you fly at night by compass, you are fine as long as you can see one star. If you lose sight of that star, you will quickly become disoriented and you won't know up from down and you will crash. With all the trees visible just below the plane, and knowing that the terrain in front of me held no sudden high hills, I had a fairly easy flight, but there were moments I wished the forward visibility would improve. It was a great relief when we finally flew out of the storm.

I heard about a pilot from Bella Coola who wanted to go to a party in Williams Lake. He flew about halfway there but had to turn back because of the weather. The saying goes that doctors don't make good pilots because they like to fly to some relaxing place for the weekend, and they have to be back Monday morning to look after their patients, which puts pressure on them to fly even when the weather is marginal. The pilot from Bella Coola waited as long as he could for the weather to improve, and no doubt got the latest weather report from the airport in Williams Lake. Finally he took off in his second attempt. The weather was passable to the Chilcotin country but socked in on him before he got to the Fraser River. By now it was also getting later in the day, which made visibility even worse. The fellow would have had few options to save himself. Finally he lost visual contact with the ground and went into a spiral dive. He must have had a very tense last few seconds. Floyd Vaughan told me once that accidents only happen to other flyers. I guess that is a good philosophy.

On one of my fur-buying trips in the east Chilcotin and Nazko areas, I flew fairly close to Quesnel. As it was getting late in the afternoon and I was getting tired, I decided to stop there for the

Lashaway Alec and his wife hold sacks of beaver pelts that I had just purchased from them in the Nazko. In the spring I often used wheels on the plane instead of skis.

night. Quesnel has some mills very close to the airport. These mills give off a lot of smoke that seems to bring on fog when air conditions are just right. Quesnel Airport is right beside the Fraser River, whereas the Williams Lake Airport is several hundred feet higher and back from the Fraser, so it doesn't accumulate fog as readily as Quesnel Airport.

One winter a few years before this trip, I had flown into Quesnel from Williams Lake with my son, Chuck, and when I got to the airport the southern approach was completely clear but the landing strip itself was covered in fog. Visibility on the strip was zero. I had plenty of room to land on the approach, but to taxi to the tie-downs I had to get Chuck to run ahead of the plane and guide me as I taxied along. The morning after staying in Quesnel on this particular fur-buying jaunt, I took a taxi from my hotel to the airport to get my plane and fly back to Anahim Lake. From the taxi I could see that there was an impenetrable layer of fog to the west of the Fraser River as far as the eye could see. The river itself was clear. I got the weather report from the airport on my arrival and learned that there was unlimited visibility and a high ceiling from Nazko to the Rainbow Mountains, so my only obstacle was the fog between here and Nazko.

Bob and Francie trapped in the mountains south of Charlotte Lake. I would meet them at Charlotte Lake to buy their fur.

As I got my plane gassed up and ready to go, I noticed that the fog around the river was pretty well stationary. This was good news, as I would have to fly north up this river to the Blackwater River, and I didn't want fog closing in behind me. I took off at the airport and flew north over the Fraser to see if the fog had enveloped the Blackwater River. There was plenty of room flying up the Fraser. The ceiling wasn't high but it was more than adequate. When I got to the Blackwater, I was pleased to see that the fog had formed over it the same as on the Fraser, the only difference being it was a much, much smaller river.

I flew up this river crowding one side, to give myself more room to manoeuvre in case an unexpected fog bank came up in front of me and I had to do a quick 180-degree turn. The farther I flew up the river, the narrower it got. I flew as slow as I could to give me more time to take evasive action if I had to. I knew the river had no 90-degree bends in it, or any big waterfalls where the land in front of me would suddenly be elevated. I was virtually flying in a flat-bottomed tunnel—the frozen river below me and the fog stretched from shore to shore over the plane. Fortunately the fog was high enough over the river to keep me safely above the trees. But I was a little worried that my tunnel was going to get smaller and smaller.

It is said that to survive flying you have to have a little yellow streak up your back. About the time I thought of this I broke into the Nazko Valley. The weather information I had received at Quesnel Airport had been correct. It was a beautiful, clear sunny day. Despite the sweating I did on my way up the Blackwater River in a tunnel of fog, before bursting into the wide blue yonder, this trip remains one of my fondest flying memories.

Slim Shirk was taking off on a rough piece of land on the Gang Ranch when something went very wrong with his engine. He shut the engine down instantly but still managed to run over it before coming to a stop. The prop had broken and had torn the engine out of the plane. A rider later found the broken part of the propeller far from the accident scene. Slim was unhurt.

A Norwegian and his friend were discussing an air battle they had been in. The Norwegian said, "There was a Fokker on my left, two Fokkers in front of me, and two more Fokkers on my right." "But they weren't Folkers," his friend said. "They were Messerschmitts." "I know," said the Norwegian, "but those Fokkers were flying those Messerschmitts."

♠

Flying and playing poker have much more in common than most people would dream of. Flying has been described as hours of boredom punctuated by moments of stark terror. I can attest to this. When I had to go on a flight lasting an hour and a half or more, over country I'd seen many times before, which was usually the case, I would take a newspaper or something else to read. Once you have climbed to the desired altitude and you are going on the proper heading, you do not need to watch every minute. The chances of someone else doing the same thing and coming in your direction are extremely remote. You are supposed to fly at different altitudes for different directions.

In poker you can get a streak of bad cards and have to throw your cards away hand after hand. This is very boring and can go on for hours or even days. I never played for more than I could afford to lose, but some people do, and that is where the moments of stark terror come in.

Mike Grenby wrote an article in the *Vancouver Sun* in 1986, saying that Brian Purdy, a chartered accountant in Williams Lake, had said that I would play any game you can name for any amount you can count. That is not correct. If some rich dude came in and wanted to flip me for ten thousand dollars, I would put that in the same category as dangerous flying. I wouldn't do it. But if I were challenged to flip for a thousand dollars, that would be like waving a mink skin when I was flying around buying fur. I would have accepted the challenge in a heartbeat.

Flying is said to be not inherently dangerous, but unforgiving of foolishness or carelessness. Poker is argued to be not gambling, but a game of skill. Poker is not inherently dangerous either, but it will not tolerate foolishness for long without causing much anguish.

The flying I did was usually short hops around the country, and there was always action when I landed—no boredom. In poker the experts say the longest you can play at a stretch is about four hours before you start losing your power of concentration and your skill level drops. Poker players almost always exceed this limit, and sometimes they play so long that it is hard on their health. I limit my poker hours when I play in big tournaments so I can play refreshed and enjoy myself and have a better chance of winning. Similarly, when I was flying I had no desire to take long trips that bored and tired me.

One day while I was flying with a passenger, Lorraine Holte, in the back seat, I turned to talk to her and noticed that her hair was blowing in the breeze coming through the gaps where the door closed onto the body of the plane. It was not the first time I had noticed the Super Cub wasn't built for comfort, but this convinced me it was time to try another type of plane.

I had read quite a bit about the Citabria. Like the Super Cub, it had a 150-horsepower Lycoming engine, and all the stats I could find indicated that it would perform pretty well on par with the Super Cub. In 1975, I sold the Cub to Roger Pentacost, who had purchased the Cless Pocket Ranch, and bought a new Citabria for fifteen thousand dollars US.

The Citabria proved to be a very good bush plane and much more comfortable than the Cub, though nothing could outperform the Cub. *Citabria* spelled backwards is *airbatic*, and I was soon to

Peter Alexis and his wife Minnie did their travelling by team and wagon.

learn what this meant. Late one afternoon I was flying back over Anahim Lake with Floyd Vaughan in the back seat, having picked him up at Peter Alexis's place on the Blackwater River. Floyd, a commercial bush pilot who flew out of Nimpo Lake for Wilderness Airlines, owned by Daniel and Gideon Schuetze, had gone through the ice with his plane and had done a little prop damage. When we were over Anahim Lake he invited me to show him how the plane performed, and he asked whether I had ever done a loop. I told him I hadn't, but had read about how to do it. Floyd had a lot more training than I did, so I attempted the loop. I lowered the nose to gain speed for the climb up to the top of the loop, and I was doing fine until I got upside down and got us into a spin. All the maps and paraphernalia got sucked out of the compartment beside me and went flying into the back of the plane. Fortunately the Citabria has flight-control instruments in both the front and back seats, and Floyd got us out of the mess using the stick in the back seat. After that he didn't ask me for any more demonstrations.

The seed was sown, however, and I wanted more flying lessons. The first chance I got (in 1975), I went to Abbotsford to get instruction in aerobatics. I learned to do loops, barrel rolls, snap rolls and wing-overs. Barrel rolls are nice, easy 360-degree rolls.

The appropriately named snap roll snaps you through 360 degrees. In the wing-over, you dive the plane for speed, then pull it almost straight up, but leaning slightly to the side you plan to come down on. Just before you stall, you give full rudder and fall into the lean. This was one of the neatest manoeuvres I did. On the way down you pull off power immediately to avoid a buildup of speed.

One day my instructor took me up in a Decathlon. This plane has a 180-horsepower Lycoming engine in it and, as I was later to learn, was an absolute dream to fly. We did a few of our simple aerobatic manoeuvres and he asked me if I would like to see an inverted stall. It was fine with me. He said he would need an extra thousand feet of altitude, and when we got there, he turned the plane upside down in a steep climbing attitude. To stall a plane when it is right side up, you pull the stick back, and when you are upside down, you push the stick forward. This he did, and I found out why we needed the extra thousand feet. We dropped upside down like a rocket. Of course he had undoubtedly done this manoeuvre dozens of times and had no trouble getting back to a normal flying attitude. But it was a manoeuvre a novice like me wouldn't be doing in Anahim Lake. I was twenty years too old to become a fighter pilot.

When I got back to Anahim Lake after my lessons, I often practised some aerobatic manoeuvres when I wasn't delivering groceries. In talking to the pilots from the States who stopped at the store, I heard of two Citabrias that had had wing failures in aerobatic manoeuvres. Shortly after that I saw an advertisement for a used Decathlon in Ontario. I phoned the owner and we made a deal to meet in Calgary and trade airplanes. I took Bud Bishop, the local RCMP officer, along for the ride. We completed the deal at the Calgary airport, then Bud and I got into the Decathlon for our return flight. The first thing I noticed was there were no earphones and I couldn't hear the tower very well. As I taxied toward the main runway, I could see a four-engine monster making a landing in front of me, and I could hear the tower talking to the pilot. The tower told him that they had a Decathlon taxiing for takeoff and weren't sure what it was going to do. They didn't have to worry about me getting in the way of that plane. When I got takeoff clearance, Bud and I headed for the Rocky Mountains and home.

For a pilot whose experience has all been flying over lakes and rivers and jackpine trees, flying over the Rockies is a learning experience. There was an endless sea of mountain peaks, some obscured by cloud. The one thing I was sure of was that the direction to take was west. When we finally got through the mountains, we flew over a little landing strip with two or three airplanes on it. As I only knew approximately where we were, I landed and obtained enough information by looking inside one of the planes to determine our location and plot a course for home.

I was very interested in flying different airplanes when I was buying fur in the bush, a lot like a kid in a candy store. Some people are like that with cars and motorcycles, but cars never particularly interested me. I didn't know how many cylinders or how much horsepower my vehicle had, but I usually knew what colour it was. One day I walked out of the store and climbed into my yellow pickup. There was some mail on the seat beside me, and when I started looking through it I noticed everything was addressed to Lloyd and Betty Norton. Before I could figure out what their mail was doing in my pickup, I realized it was their pickup. Fortunately this was an easy matter to correct on the ground.

The Decathlon was a beautiful plane to fly. It didn't have the liftoff of the Super Cub or the Citabria, but after making a delivery out in the bush, I would come home over Anahim Lake with an empty plane with 180 horsepower that was stressed at 9 Gs, positive and negative. This meant the top of the wing would take as much pressure as the bottom of the wing. I would fly twenty feet above the fence and follow the curves as close as I could. Coming up to the trees dividing Anahim Lake, I would pull up just over the treetops, then drop down the other side over the lake. The plane would make just as sharp a turn as you wanted to pull it around, and climb as steep as was comfortable. I had more fun flying this plane than anything else I ever did.

I was also finding that aerobatics and freighting weren't so compatible. The plane always had oats or something spilled in it. Two aerobatic pilots I had read a lot about and seen perform at different air shows I had gone to, had both been killed. These two men were the best of the best pilots. One of these pilots, Art Scholl, was practising manoeuvres off the coast of California when he radioed to his base that he was in trouble, no doubt in one of his aerobatic configurations. And then he radioed that he was really in trouble. Neither he nor his plane was ever found.

One day in winter I knocked an accumulation of ice off the wings of the Decathlon and went full power down the strip for takeoff, but the plane wouldn't lift off. I stopped and taxied back to where I had started and found another coat of clear ice I hadn't seen the first time. Not many days after this I took off with a load that was a little heavier than usual. At the west end of the strip, the road to Bella Coola runs past the Department of Highways shop. On takeoff I flew down past the shop considerably lower than the trees beside the road and was unable to gain altitude. I must have lost what is called ground effect—the wings compress the air against the strip and give lift, which of course you lose once you're off the ground. I was able to nudge the plane with the right rudder enough to get over Little Anahim Lake and gain enough speed so I could climb. I told Floyd Vaughan about this one day when I ran into him and he said it wouldn't have mattered whether I pulled the stick back or pushed it forward, the plane would have gone down.

One day early in the winter, when I was taking off from Antoine Baptiste's place east of Tsacha Lake, there was such a lack of snow that I hit a hummock hard enough to break off the right landing gear. I had just assessed the damage when William Cassam came along on his way home on a snow machine. He lived on the western end of Tsacha Lake on the Blackwater River. I hitched a ride behind him to Jim and Paddy Chadwell's place, where I phoned home on their radiophone. Then I had supper with Chadwells, and we were sitting around relaxing when we heard the rumble of a very big plane. I had heard it before and knew it was Search and Rescue

William Cassam and his daughter Ronnie receive a load of supplies in the Blackwater.

from Comox. The jar that had broken my landing gear had set off my emergency location transmitter, and a Russian satellite had picked up the distress signal and alerted Search and Rescue. As the plane circled over the house, we tried to talk to them on Chadwell's radio, but the batteries in the radio went dead. They circled over the house in the pitch-black night and used their searchlight to drop us another radio. To do this from an airplane of that size was damned professional to say the least. We finally convinced them that nobody was hurt and they turned and headed back to their base. Search and Rescue has to be one of the greatest services the country has to offer. Floyd Vaughan picked me up the next day and flew me back to the store. My insurance company took care of the plane, and I soon had it back working again.

As I became more and more interested in airplanes, I figured I should take a scientific approach and find out more about what makes them fly. To understand it, I knew I would have to keep it very simple. First I studied the composition of a wing. If you

Jim, Paddy and their daughter unload their groceries at Twin Lakes in the Blackwater.

imagine a line from the leading edge to the trailing edge of the wing, you have what is called the chord. The part of the wing above the chord is the upper camber, or curve, and the part below the chord is the lower camber. I knew that when you increase the upper camber, you increase the wing's lift capabilities, but I didn't know why. Then I ran across Bernoulli's principle. This wise man proved that air pressure decreases when air moves faster. When you increase the camber or curvature on top of the wing relative to the camber on the bottom of the wing, the air has to move faster to get over the wing than the air moving under the wing. The pressure on top of the wing drops, and as the air moves slower on the bottom of the wing, it produces more pressure and therefore lift. The angle of the wing as it moves through the air is known as the angle of attack, and it produces more and more lift the faster the plane goes.

Another important part of the formula is the pitch of the propeller, which determines how big a bite of air it takes per revolution.

When Slim Shirk was teaching me to fly the Cessna 150, it seemed to take forever to lift off. There were times when I thought one of us would have to get out and run alongside the plane until it finally took off. One day I went for my lesson and was amazed at the plane's performance. I thought Slim must have put a new engine in it, but he had changed the propeller to one with a finer pitch.

My Super Cub and Citabria both had a well-cambered wing for bush flying, plus they both had flaps, a hinged part of the inner wing. When the flaps are lowered by the pilot, they increase the camber of the wing, adding to the lift and how slow the plane can fly. The advantage the Decathlon had over these planes was 30 horsepower and a constant-speed prop. That allows the pilot to change the pitch of the prop to fine pitch for takeoff and course pitch for cruising, something like changing gears in a car. These advantages were overshadowed by no flaps and a symmetrical wing—the upper and lower cambers were the same, which made the plane weak on lift, though the shape of the Decathlon wing made for smooth flying. To fly any plane safely, its limitations and capabilities must be known and respected.

So I began to think that I shouldn't be trying to make a bush plane out of a Decathlon, I should buy a Bellanca Scout instead. The Scout is like the Citabria except it has a double seat behind the pilot and a 180-horsepower Lycoming engine. I had read a lot about this plane and knew it would be good for my business, mainly because it would haul bigger loads and it had the get-up-and-go that I needed.

By this time the fur part of my store business was booming. Fur was high-priced and all the trappers were after it. I knew they made Bellanca Scouts with long-range tanks, and if I bought one, it would double the area I could cover in buying fur, and my business would be twice as interesting because I would be dealing with many more interesting people. I phoned Wes Carter, a good friend in Amboy, Washington. Wes used to fly into Pan Phillips's fishing lodge fairly often, and he finally bought a small acreage there. We had some great poker games at Pan's. I told Wes what I wanted and

This is my Scout on Qualcho Lake. Flying in the wilderness and meeting trappers on days like this can't be beat.

asked him to keep his eyes open for a deal on one. Before long he found the plane I was looking for, and I extended my fur-buying range north of Ootsa Lake, beyond Babine to Takla Lake, and as far west as Bear Lake. To the east of Takla Lake I went down to Trembler Lake, Stewart Lake and on to Fort St. James.

On my first trip farther north I plotted a course to the northwest corner of Takla Lake, and I just happened to land at Johnny French's. Johnny and his wife had a large family and I think they were all trappers catching fur in that huge country. I had certainly hit the right spot for fur buying. The Frenches were very hospitable people and I stayed with them that night. In the next couple of days I met many local trappers, all Natives except for Ray Pollard, who had married Lil French, Johnny's daughter. Ray had a place where the Cottonwood River flowed into the west end of Takla Lake.

Having bought all the fur I could shake up, I flew down the lakes to Fort St. James and bought fur at the Pinchi and Tachi reserves on my way. As it would not be wise or convenient to carry cash to buy fur, I wrote cheques for all my purchases. One trapper at Tachi looked at me and said, "Maybe I should feengerprint you before you go."

Over the years I made many trips to this great country and had a very high regard for the people I met there. Eventually I became known from one end of it to the other as the flying fur buyer. One reason, no doubt, was because who could remember a name like D'Arcy Christensen?

On one trip I stayed overnight with Ray and Lil Pollard, and at night the wolves serenaded up the Cottonwood Canyon. This was real wilderness. The next morning I flew northwest to a trapper's cabin on Bear Lake, the end of the line for the railway that the Social Credit government had built to nowhere from Fort St. James. When I landed on Bear Lake and got to the cabin, I walked down a shovelled path to get to the door. This was very deep-snow country. The caribou and moose here had suffered a terrible toll when the railway came through. When they got caught on the track, there was just no escape. The snow was too deep and trains don't stop easily.

In this big northern country, someone always seemed to have drowned doing something on the lakes. A doctor from Fort St. James was canoeing on Stewart Lake when his canoe tipped over,

Horses wait to transport Francis Cassam and his granddaughter, along with newly purchased sacks of oats, to their home in the Blackwater.

Snow machines, skis and an airplane—Who could ask for more?
L to R: unidentified lady, Howard Prosser, Roger Williams sitting on a snow machine and Kris by the skis.

and he couldn't get back to it because he had Parkinson's disease. A man was moving a bulldozer along the shoreline of Stewart Lake and decided to take a shortcut over the ice. It didn't hold him up, and he drowned. Early one winter the Natives at the Tachi Reserve told me they had spent much of the summer looking for the body of a man who had drowned. Early one winter another young man on a snow machine decided to test the ice on the southwest side of Stewart Lake. He intended to go a short distance from shore and turn around and come back, but the ice broke when he turned, and he drowned in front of his family. A man on Babine Lake decided to take no chances so he towed a rowboat behind his snowmobile. He went through the ice, and the snow machine sunk the boat he was towing, but somehow he lived to tell the tale.

On a flight northeast of Anahim Lake to pick up fur, when I still had the Citabria, I received word that P.L. West wanted a ride back to Anahim. P.L. was a Native Ulkatcho man who lived on the local reserve. I found him easily and landed in a very strong but favourable wind. When I got out of the plane to load him and his belongings, I noticed the wind was howling down a fairly high hill that I had landed toward. There were hills on either side of me running toward the hill in front of me. I had plenty of room in front to take off but not enough room to go over that hill. I didn't like the idea of trying to fly over the hills on either side in such a strong wind, so I took off straight toward the hill. I climbed as high as I could and raised the nose in a very steep climb, and as the plane slowed down I kicked into full rudder. The nose of the plane swapped ends with the tail and we were going back in the direction we had come from, and we passed the hill on our left like a bullet. As Howard Prosser would have said, we were out of there like a mallard duck kicked in the ass. I had been so involved in taking off I had forgotten about P.L. in the back seat. Now I turned my head and asked him how he was doing. He said that was the scaredest ride he had ever had. That was the only time I ever used an aerobatic manoeuvre in normal flying. It had worked perfectly but it was hard on my passenger.

One year I flew a Native trapper named Patrick William Jack up to Ootsa Lake with his provisions to go trapping. I was on

Pat Sill drives his wagon with wife Minnie and mother-in-law Mary Joe Cahoose. Near Anahim Lake.

wheels and landed on the ice that was blown clear of snow. When we landed, the wind was just howling down this big lake. As it was snowing a bit and getting late in the day, I decided to spend the night with Patrick. I chopped shallow holes in the ice under the wheels of my plane, and tied the tail to a good tree. Patrick and I made our way off the lake to a more sheltered spot in the timber. I lit a small fire and he went to get some blankets that he kept in a tourist's summer cabin not far away. When he got back it was very dark, but we managed to find a couple of fairly comfortable places to sleep. He gave me some of the blankets and took some for himself. When I awoke the next morning I saw that Patrick had given me three-quarters of the blankets, and that was barely enough to keep me warm. He never told me how he slept that night, but I will always remember his generosity. Patrick took his own life some years later, for reasons I don't know. During that night out by Ootsa Lake, I couldn't have asked for better company. I didn't know Patrick well but I never heard him complain about anything. This was his home.

On my Ootsa Lake run at Grassy Plains, I used to stop and pick up John Jack, a young Native man who lived there with his parents. Sometimes John would drive me around in his pickup to collect

Marilyn Sill looks happy with the family's winter catch of fur.

Buying fur in Grassy Plains from John Jack's sister, Ann, and her husband Billy.

furs. One afternoon I was going to land on a hill close to his place, just below the main road. I looked the hill over carefully, picked a spot to land and made a good approach, but when I touched down I hit a much steeper slope than was indicated by my aerial view. The right ski broke through the snow and turned me sharply into the slope I was landing on. The plane came to an abrupt stop, but the impact snapped the right spring-steel landing gear in half. The snow was so deep, no other damage was done to the plane. I shovelled the snow away from the plane, determined what tools I would need to remove the broken landing gear, and snowshoed up to the road. When I got there a vehicle had stopped and a guy was waiting for me. He told me he had seen the plane but didn't know how it had got there as he couldn't see any tracks where it had landed. He gave me a ride to a little store owned by two brothers by the name of Coombs. These brothers were very knowledgeable about a lot of things and I wished I had more time to talk with them. They drove me down the road to the plane with enough tools to take the landing gear off. It was dark and damned cold by the time I got the gear off and went back up to the road. When we got back to the store, my hands started to warm up, and each finger felt like it had a toothache. I had worked in a lot of cold weather but nothing like this. I guess it was the combination of cold steel and cold temperatures.

For a
Flying Fur Buyer
phone ONE D
Anahim Lake.

A. C. CHRISTENSEN

Passing over Little Anahim Lake,
I put the full flaps on to slow the plane
down for the photo on this poster.

We took the landing gear to the sawmill and a welder there made an excellent job of welding it back together. The next day after buying fur, I got the gear back on my plane and was on my way.

On one of my flying excursions near Nazko, I bought a fisher skin from a young paleface trapper. He had caught this fisher on another person's property and he showed me a signed note from that person, giving him permission to keep the fisher. Two weeks later I was paid a visit by a game warden from Quesnel. According to his record book I had bought the fisher skin illegally, and he wanted me to sign a paper to this effect. This version of things and the way he confronted me made it seem that I was in the wrong. I wondered why he didn't give me notice of my legal rights, and why he had driven all the way from Quesnel to Anahim Lake to make trouble over a seventy-dollar fisher skin when I was buying thousands of dollars' worth of fur every month. Smelling a rat, I told the guy I would sign nothing and would take the matter to court.

A couple of weeks later I had to fly to Quesnel and appear before a judge. It soon became apparent the case wasn't going in the game warden's favour, so he told the judge he needed more time. This meant I would have to fly back to Anahim Lake, then go back to Quesnel later for another hearing. The original judge wouldn't hear the case again, saying that he would be prejudiced. A second judge heard the case and I was exonerated.

The game warden was trying to make a name for himself by

Pan and I meet up with Anne (John Jack's wife) and her young son Billy at the Vanderhoof rodeo.

giving me a bad mark, as I was known all over the country as the "flying fur buyer." I don't know how much the procedure cost me and the court system, but it was a lot more than the worth of the seventy-dollar fisher skin.

Buying fur wasn't like flipping a coin for double or nothing. You really had to know a lot about many different kinds of fur. For the first few years I wasn't too knowledgeable. When fur prices were low, this didn't show up too drastically. But as fur became much more valuable, I really had to know what I was doing. I used to ship fur to the Western Canadian Raw Fur auction sales, founded by Teddy Pappas Sr., and in my day run by his son, Teddy Pappas Jr. I visited their place of business in Vancouver several times. Teddy Jr. would personally give me a tour through all the fur that they were receiving for their next sale, or he would get Tommy, one of his main fur graders, to show me the fur. They taught me what to look for in every species for the highest value, and they showed me what was going wrong with every skin they had. I soon became much more proficient at buying fur.

When prices were sky high, everybody wanted to get in on the act. I was flying so much of the time that I had to protect my fur-buying business at the store. I would strip a bunch of fur from all the best pelts and get someone to take the inferior fur and sell it to one of the other businesses. Beavers rub the guard hairs off their backs toward spring, which can quarter their value. Otters get singed from too much sun, and the ends of their hairs curl. Coyotes, foxes and wolves shed their fur. When lynx fur was very high, I could get a thousand dollars for one skin if the underbelly hair was thick and long and silky. Unrubbed beaver hit a hundred dollars. A fur buyer who doesn't have a lot of this kind of information was in an ocean of trouble. I did have it, and eventually I became the only fur buyer in the area, and definitely the only flying fur buyer.

Years after I left the fur-buying business, Kris and the kids and I took a trip to Las Vegas. On the flight back, I put on my headphones, turned on the radio, flicked through the stations and came across the tower talking to the pilot of the plane. The tower was giving the captain exact instructions, and I got totally absorbed in it. I knew what the plane was going to do before it did it, and I could tell Kris and kids what was going to happen. It was almost like I was flying the plane. At one point I looked up and realized that half the people on the plane were listening to me saying what the plane was going to do next. I was amazed by this way of controlling traffic. As we got out of range of one station, another would take over. When we got close to the airport, the pilot was told what speed to fly, what heading to take and what altitude to fly at. These three parameters changed constantly as we neared the strip. I could see that this was a very safe and effective way of handling a large volume of traffic coming into an airport. It was a lot different than flying in the bush.

♠ WILLIE SULIN

Willie Sulin was an Ulkatcho game guide and tracker from Towdystan, a small parcel of reserve land three or four miles south of Nimpo Lake. He was known as an astute tracker, and once he became the talk of the town.

In the early 1980s a young mentally disabled man named Tory Jack, son of Gene Jack and his wife Ideela (who died giving birth to

Tory), decided to take a jaunt out in the wilderness. He walked away from the home of his grandmother, Susan Cahoose, at Fish Trap on the Ulkatcho reserve, with a plan to walk to Anahim Lake, some ten miles away. He didn't tell anyone where he was going, and by the time he was missed he was several miles from Susan's house. A big search party was organized, and the police and Search and Rescue were notified. Before long, a large part of the local population was looking for Tory.

Willie Sulin: Tracker extraordinaire.
PHOTO SAGE BIRCHWATER.

Susan headed up a base camp for the searchers about a dozen miles east of Anahim Lake. This was the last place Tory's tracks had been spotted. For a week searchers combed the area using planes and ground parties on foot, but they came up with no results. Then Willie Sulin and his horse arrived to join the search. Willie knew that a lost person will sometimes become disoriented and scared, and will hide from searchers. On his first day, Willie spotted Tory's boot tracks in the mud so he figured he was on his trail. The second day he noticed his horse's ears prick up as he entered a small string of meadows on the edge of the jackpine forest. Willie looked in the direction his horse's ears were pointing and spotted Tory sitting on a log at the far end of the meadow. At the same time, Tory saw the man on horseback and took off like a shot into the bush. Willie shouted out, "Tory!" and the young guy stopped running. "Oh, you!" Tory replied, once he had recognized Willie.

For the next little while people couldn't stop talking about Willie and the unique way he used his horse to find a missing boy who

Dave Gladdin and Don Woodward were characters that you had to meet, but should never attempt to understand.

had been lost in the bush for more than a week. Willie told me later, "I don't find Tory, my horse he find him." No further explanation was needed. It took an extraordinary tracker to follow the signs and notice where his horse was looking, and to find one lone person in a wilderness as vast as that one.

Tory took off again a few years later, and despite a summer-long search by members of the Ulkatcho community, no trace of him was ever found.

♠ ROGER PENTACOST

Roger Pentacost, who bought the Cless Pocket Ranch and my Super Cub, was a moneyed man from England. He and his wife Marguerite had managed to squirrel a considerable number of pounds out of the motherland when they came to Canada. I got to know them quite well and we became good friends. One winter Roger had John Siebert as his ranch manager. Siebert had a lot of experience with ranching and cattle and had a good reputation. Early in the winter the Cless Pocket Ranch used one of its meadows, called the Blainey Meadow after a Native resident who was gone before my day, for rustling the cattle before hay had to be fed. Blainey Meadow bordered Anahim Lake west of Cless Pocket Ranch. The ice on this part of the lake was treacherous, and cattle were always watered in a creek that ran past the meadow. The animals had to be watched carefully. One winter day when Siebert had several hundred head of Pentacost's cattle rustling on Blainey Meadow, they somehow got out on the ice looking for water, and the ice gave way as all the cattle crowded in. When this tragedy was finally contained, over a hundred head of cattle had drowned. The dead animals had to be pulled out of the lake by tractors, towed to the north side of the meadow into the timber, and burned. It must have been a hell of a job. I ran into Siebert when he was on his way to phone Roger and tell him the bad news. That also must have been a hell of a job.

Roger and I kidded each other a lot, especially about money. He stood in a much deeper green than I ever did, and at times he would save himself a few dollars where nobody else would dare to go. Once when he and Marguerite came to Anahim Lake for the annual Stampede and were camped in my yard beside the store, they ran out of ketchup. Roger came into my house with his empty ketchup bottle and took enough of my ketchup to do him for their stay. The store was only a hundred feet away and was well stocked with ketchup.

By this time Roger had gotten out of the ranching business in Anahim Lake and had purchased a farm in Chilliwack. One fall he phoned me and invited me to go down for a poker game with some of his buddies. I flew to Cache Creek, got bluffed out by the weather and hitchhiked the rest of the way. When I finally arrived at the house he had built, I realized that building castles is partially hereditary. It took me several minutes to find a way to get into the mansion. We had a good poker game, and Roger and Marguerite were excellent hosts.

On one of his trips to Anahim Lake, Roger got interested in a sauna I had put in a spare room in the store. I needed the room for the store, so I sold him the sauna. The deal was I was to deliver it to him when I got the chance. He had sold his Chilliwack property and had purchased a fairly big piece of property near Armstrong, where I delivered the sauna and had an enjoyable stay with him and his wife. When it came time for me to go he said he would mail me a cheque later on. This was fine with me, except "later on" got later and later. I phoned him a couple of times and mentioned that "later on" had long since come and gone. I finally decided that he was stalling the payment to collect the little bit of interest he would make by keeping the money in the bank. We were good friends, but neither one of us would let the other get away with something like this. I somehow got hold of the small claims court where he was living and for a joke turned the matter over to them. A week or ten days later I got a phone call. As soon as I picked up the phone, all I could hear was a mad Englishman swearing on the other end of the line. He yelled, "Dossy, you dirty bossted, Dossy, you dirty bossted." By the time the last "dirty bossted" came out I was just about breaking a gut laughing. The small claims court had done its job.

STARTS & ENDS

I MET WES CARTER AT PAN PHILLIPS'S FISHING LODGE IN THE early 1970s. He used to fly up from Amboy, Washington, in his Cessna 180, and sometimes he would bring his friends, Olly Moody, Steve Lynes or anyone else who wanted to go for a ride. Two of his other comrades, Mike Baker and Jerry Davis, used to come in their own planes. Wes bought a small acreage on the west side of a hill bordering Pan's fishing lodge, and I ran into him quite often at Pan's when I stopped to deliver Pan's mail. It wasn't long before Wes and I got into some serious poker games.

Wes was a big man, probably 250 pounds. He seldom drank booze, but when he did drink, he didn't stop until he was totally obliterated. I was selling gas at the airport in Anahim Lake around this time, and when Wes would gas up we always flipped double or nothing for his gas. I never kept track of the wins or losses—it would have to come out pretty even. What I did notice was that it got harder and harder to steal his quarter.

Wes had one of the biggest plumbing contracting businesses in his area of Washington State. He once did a hundred houses for the US Army that were later barged to Alaska. I always seemed to be buying or selling pieces of real estate around the country, and when I visited him in Amboy, he showed me some of his very nice rental and development properties. One day in 1976 when Wes flew in from Pan's he said he was pretty keen on buying the

L to R: Pan, Wes Carter, Ollie Moodie, Wes's wife Georgia and their son on one of Pan and my visits to Wes's home in Amboy, Washington.

C2 Ranch. This ranch, ten or twelve miles east of Anahim Lake, had been started by my cousin John Clayton (named after his and my grandfather) years earlier. Since then it had had a few different owners and a fair number of improvements done to it. It was a pretty good ranch. We decided on a price we would pay for it and bought it, and I was back in the ranching business again. The poker games at Pan's had gotten pretty big and I wound up with a half-interest in a considerable amount of ranch equipment, including tractors. Financing the rest of my half of the operation was not too difficult. Wes didn't have to finance his half of the ranch, so we were in business.

How I was going to run a ranch with three hundred head on it, besides the other activities I had going, I never even considered. I didn't have an overabundance of cash but I always seemed to have a surplus of energy. We had to complete some fences in our holdings and extend some drainage ditches on the main meadow. Two ranch houses and good corrals were already built, and we had more tractors and haying equipment than we could use.

But ranching was tougher now than it used to be. Prices were high, and cattle were susceptible to pneumonia, diphtheria and other sicknesses. This was unheard of when I had last ranched. We had to give the animals so many shots and medicines that I almost quit eating meat.

The store was in fine shape. It was paid off and I had a good crew running it. Nestor Malinsky and his son-in-law, Jordi Tubbs, were both meat cutters, and Wendy Little, Kris Mutrie and my bookkeeper, Janet Prosser, took turns running the till. We had fresh produce, milk, hardware, dry goods, animal feed, books and magazines. Everything you would expect in a country store. A sign outside the store said it all: "If we don't have it, you don't need it."

In September 1980, my daughter Andrea came with me on a flight to the Blackwater. On the way back we came around the Ilgachuz Mountains and up the Dean River toward the town of Anahim Lake, and from ten miles out we could see there was a huge fire in town. It was nearly dusk, so we also noticed that all the lights were out. When we finally reached the edge of town we saw that it was

Wendy Leon (Tommy Holt's daughter) serves Johnny and Mary-Lou Blackwell's son, Sydney. On the far right is Jim Akins—a noted cook and a man who could talk continuously.

our store that had burned, and now it was a pile of smoking rubble. We had left a load of clothes in the dryer and apparently something had gone wrong with the dryer belt or bearings, and had started the fire.

Louise Moxon, who lived a short distance down the road from the store with her husband, Cammy, wrote a poem to commemorate the store and mourn its loss.

> *A famous landmark*
> *Has left our street.*
> *It stood for years*
> *On shaky feet.*
>
> *This old building*
> *Contained much history,*
> *And much of its contents*
> *Will remain a mystery.*
>
> *If you paid cash or charged it up,*
> *The service was the same—*
> *Delivery by truck or air,*
> *That's what brought it fame.*
>
> *The customer's cry:*
> *"Where shall we go?"*
> *Not down the street,*
> *Their prices aren't low;*
> *The owners are cranky*
> *And their service is slow.*
>
> *With his politician's smile*
> *and a wave of his hand,*
> *D'Arcy boldly stated,*
> *We're going to rebuild*
> *Where it used to stand.*
>
> *Before you know it*
> *We'll be back to work,*
> *If I can get these kids*
> *Not to shirk.*

We'll build with brick
And cement too,
Totally designed
By a Norwegian Jew.

The contractor's coming
In a week or a day,
If only the insurance
Will decide to pay.

We'll be back in business
Before too long
If things go right
And don't go wrong.

Just keep in mind
A.C.C.,
Where prices are cheap
And the coffee is free.

As soon as possible I had a contractor outfit from Bella Coola put up a block building with no windows. Windows are points of entry for thieves and they take up wall space that is needed to display merchandise. Clarence Hall did the block work and Lloyd Norton was the main carpenter for the woodwork. Lloyd's daughter, Ami, clerked for me in the store for a fair length of time.

Before it burned, the old store had become too small and was inefficient to run. In a way I was lucky to have to build a modern store in its place. But the old store had some interesting curios hanging on the walls that were lost in the fire. We had some genetically modified fur, including a white squirrel, whose chance of surviving would have been slight. We had collected moose feet with toes grown so long and curled up that the animal would hardly have been able to walk, a condition that must have been caused by the moose foundering on too much rich food. I had also bought Ed Collet's old saddle from Tim Draney and hung it up as a keepsake. Ed and Tim had been partners in a cattle ranch at Lily Lake, after

My old store had pretty much served its purpose by the time it burnt down in 1980. The new store was more modern and much easier to run.

which Ed worked at the Cless Pocket Ranch for a few years. He was a soft-spoken man with a good sense of humour, and he had great balance on a horse and excelled in bareback riding and steer riding. When he left Anahim he settled on a ranch near Merritt. He had always been a quiet drinker with a love for whisky, and he went out of this world indulging in his favourite pastime.

We put in a walk-in cooler, produce stands, a freezer, milk and pop coolers, a hardware display and a dry-goods section. We got the latest cash register and scales. We had a warehouse where we could unload our merchandise to be unpacked and sorted for the store. Before winter we were back in business. When buying equipment for the new store I had tried to get a scale like the one we had lost. I thought it was the cat's meow. It was a mechanical one, and when something was put on the tray to be weighed, the needle swung back and forth and finally settled on the weight. Luckily these obsolete scales were no longer available. The new ones were electronic and gave instant readings. With the volume of goods we were now moving out, you couldn't wait for a mechanical scale or anything else.

Another difference between the two stores was that the new one cost $100,000 more than the insurance we got for the old store. Interest rates were running between 18 and 20 percent. Over the next three years, everything I made went to pay bank loans and interest, and the bank I was dealing with was understandably getting a little nervous. Wes Carter and I went to see the bank about our new ranch operation. Neither of us was very impressed by the person we saw. I knew that both Johnny Blackwell and Bryce Sager, who bought the Cless Pocket Ranch, were having to finance mortgages. I talked my problems over with both of them, and sent this letter to a different bank:

> *Dear Sir:*
>
> *On Johnny Blackwell's recommendation I am send-*
> *ing you financial information on my store, ranch and*
> *personal income. I built a new store after a fire in the fall*
> *of 1980. In 1981 I paid my bank $18,242.74 in interest*
> *and bank charges. In 1982 the bill was $9,834.13 and this*
> *year it will be down to $6,600.00. I must now deal with*
> *some underling with the ass out of his pants, and can't*
> *get proper financing.*

I informed the bank of what assets from the ranch we were selling, in the form of surplus machinery, and said that I was in line to get a liquor store licence and that Carrier Lumber was going to start a sawmill in Anahim Lake, and I would need around a hundred thousand dollars. With this letter I switched my account to the other bank and never had any more trouble financing my endeavours.

Around this time a group of us poker players—Lyle Morman, Steve Suetta, Schuster Johnson, Charlie Grosso, Gabe Pinette, Mel Call, Doug Norberg and others—used to rent a room in the Chilcotin Inn in Williams Lake for some pretty lively poker games. Some big poker games get completely out of hand, where the game gets too big and exceeds what the players can afford to be playing for, and a group of us got into one that fills that description. I wound up with just over $20,000. That game ruined a good social event.

It was the end of our poker evenings in the Chilcotin Inn, which had been going on for years and were a lot of fun. But the $20,000 was good for my mortgages.

The new store was incomparably better than the old one. Business grew each year, and that was easy to handle in a bigger, more efficient store. In 1984 we got the licence to sell liquor. The markup on liquor was low but the volume was high. It only takes a few seconds to sell a fifteen-dollar bottle of liquor. We were also allowed to charge a chilling fee on beer or anything we put in the cooler. In 1985, Uwe Vullings painted a mural across the front of the store, showing two racing horses. This improved the look of the store immensely. In 1986 we won Consolidated Grocers' award for the most improved store with over two thousand square feet of selling space. The competition for this award took in several mini-markets in Williams Lake.

In 1985 pine mushrooms became a huge business in Anahim Lake. The Japanese name for this mushroom is *matsutake*, "the aroma of fall," and we couldn't get enough of them. I turned the buying of these mushrooms over to Nestor Malinsky, my store

Store staff: Gene Andrick, Nestor Malinsky, me, Nestor's son-in-law Jordi, his wife Laurie, Wendy Little and Janet Prosser.

Nestor Malinsky, the mushroom-buyer supreme, assesses the new store.

manager. He bought for a company that gave him a dollar a pound to grade them, put them in baskets and ship them to Vancouver. From there they were flown to Japan. The price of the number one mushrooms fluctuated from a few dollars to sixty dollars or more per pound. Nestor and his helpers got well paid for their efforts, and the store benefitted from the stimulus to the economy. Everybody seemed to be picking mushrooms and the money flowed like buttermilk.

One thing I had inherited when I took over the store was the accounts payable, or credit extended to customers. The Natives called it "jawbone." By any name, these accounts had to be handled delicately. You had to know how honest the person was who you were giving the jawbone to. If you gave too much credit, the person might shop elsewhere when they got money. But you couldn't just cut off someone who depended on credit, because you might leave them in a hell of a mess, or even hungry. The jawbone aspect required a lot more bookkeeping than a cash business and it was always a balancing act. If someone stuck you with a small amount of jawbone, you had to put it down as part of your tuition fee and not let it bother you.

A man and his wife were in their house one night when there was a knock on the door. The man was busy fixing the washing machine so he persuaded his wife to answer the door. As she was in the shower, she wrapped herself in a bath towel and went to the door and opened it. She saw a man standing in the doorway who had obviously come in a red pickup that was parked in the driveway. He took one look at the towel she had wrapped around her and told her he would give her eight hundred dollars if she would take it off. She thought for a second and dropped the towel. He gave her the eight hundred dollars and left.

As the wife went back into the house, her husband asked her who had come to the door. "Oh it was just someone in an old red pickup," she said. The husband said he knew who that would have been. "Did he leave you that eight hundred dollars he owed me?" he asked.

In 1987, Bill Kordyban set up a sawmill and planer mill two miles east of the town of Anahim Lake. It went under the name of Carrier Lumber. Along with the logging operation, this enterprise put the first steady payroll in town. The mill ran successfully for several years, until the local Natives decided they were getting short-changed on timber that was being logged on lands they had entitlement to. In the end, Bill Kordyban got into a shoving match with Dave Zirnhelt, Minister of Forests, over the timber rights Kordyban had already been given. The matter went to court and Kordyban was paid a substantial sum of money. When the smoke cleared, the Natives had a third of the operation, Kordyban had another third and residents of the area were allowed to buy up the remaining third. Residents were limited to $100,000 in shares. Most of the businesses, workers and residents bought up the shares. This local component of the enterprise ran successfully for a few years as CAT Resources Ltd. In 2007, the local share owners sold their shares to Carrier-Chilcotin Ventures Ltd. and to the Native interests of Yun Ka Whu'ten Development Ltd. Lumber prices have since taken a kicking and I doubt that the operation is having an easy time of it.

In 1987 my son, Chuck, who had bought a half-interest in the store in 1981, convinced me we should build a laundromat across the street from the store. We decided to put a storage rental in the bottom half of the building and a takeout café in the top half, separate from the washers and dryers. My oldest daughter, Cary, and her husband also had an interest in it. We decided to call it Lucky Flip Laundromat.

The inspector for the sewage was Kris Andrews, a lady biologist from Williams Lake with the Ministry of Environment for the region. One thing led to another and we decided to "ride the range together." Kris kept her job in Williams Lake and brought a small load of liquor to the store every other weekend. On alternate weekends I would go to Williams Lake in my pickup and bring back a much larger load. The freighting arrangement worked very well up until the store was sold.

On several occasions, Kris and I visited Wes Carter and his wife, Georgia, and their kids, Ami and Sam. Wes drove us to many

I first met Kris when she came to inspect the waterworks for the Lucky Flip Laundromat.

My son, Chuck, working on the construction of the the Lucky Flip.

interesting places near their home in the Amboy area in southern Washington State.

In summer Kris and I teamed up with Bob and June Draney, and Ken Stranaghan from Bella Coola, and we would ride into the local mountains with packhorses for a week or ten days at a time. Wes came with us two or three times and once brought Ami along.

One time Wes and I and Mike Baker flew up to Gerry Davis's fishing establishment in Alaska to fish halibut. It was a new experience for me. Gerry cooked the small fish we caught in a beer batter, and we had the best fish and chips I have ever eaten.

In 1978, Wes and I decided to sell the cows on our C2 Ranch and buy yearlings to winter and sell in the fall. This was a busy time on the ranch, and we had Pan and whoever else we could hoodwink into helping us brand and doctor the animals before winter set in.

One year Wes's big burly friend, Steve Lyons, drove up from Amboy with his wife to visit and take in the local stampede. Steve

Ken Stranaghan and I did most of the packing on our mountain trips. Kris Andrews and June Draney would carefully weigh everything to be packed. We seldom had to stop to fix a pack. PHOTO KRIS ANDREWS.

was a tough and nervy character, and he decided to smuggle in some moonshine by hiding it in a waterbed. When he got to the border on his way up, he had his wife lie down on the bed and told the border guards that she had sprained her back and couldn't sit up. They let him through. I don't know anybody else who would even try something like this. On the night of their arrival at the ranch, Steve demonstrated how drunk you could get on a bit of this stuff. I was glad it also put you to sleep. His wife put him to bed without incident, and the next morning when Wes, Olly Moody, Brian Smith, Steve and his wife, and I showed up in the ranch house for breakfast, Steve looked no worse for wear.

We had a waterbed full of alcohol on our hands and none of us had a thirst for it. It was decided that we would take a couple of mickeys of it to the stampede dance that evening. When the time arrived, Wes, Steve and I loitered outside the dance hall, generously dispensing free booze to anyone who was thirsty. Some takers had a hell of a time breathing after swallowing a little of our firewater. Others threw up immediately. One paleface with thick lips chugalugged a hefty drink and went straight into the dance. I followed him but lost him in the crowd. If he stayed on his feet, he was one tough drinker.

Back at the ranch we still had a lot of white lightning to get rid of. We got enough empty wine bottles from the store to hold what was in the waterbed. In a short while the moccasin telegraph had spread the word of our amazing inventory. We even had people fly in from Williams Lake to procure our wares. In a matter of days we were again running a dry ranch.

After four or five years of ranching, Wes and I concluded that there wasn't a whole lot of money to be made. We sold the ranch and got our money back on it. We had enjoyed a lot of action the place had provided, but it was time to stop.

Pan died in 1983, and Wes flew to the Blackwater a lot less often. After selling the ranch I didn't see him in Anahim Lake much more either. Kris and I found out on one of our trips to Amboy that someone had given Wes a hit of cocaine at a party and he was immediately hooked on it. When we were at his place he was just coming off several days of bingeing on this drug with no sleep. Gerry Davis, who was working on one of his building projects, knew Wes was occupying an old house close to where he was working. He finally figured out that Wes was on a dope binge. I had made a spoof album of me getting Wes to quit smoking and lose some weight. I had cut a lot of funny pictures out of magazines and had written short comments to go with the pictures. Wes actually did quit smoking for a while and lost some weight. He told me that during this time he felt like a young gazelle. After visiting him on that trip, it was easy to see he was in bad trouble. I wrote him a little verse in May 1992.

In ninety-one and ninety-two
Things went wrong as they sometimes do,
And Carter was to wear a very tight shoe.
Wealth came easy because of his brain,
A mansion he built with little pain.
Investments grew with no end in sight,
But something was wrong with this man of might.

Science has proven that a gene misplaced
In latter years will have to be faced.
His lust for smoke from birth was got
By a genetic quirk that would cost him a lot.
He smoked and he ate as he watched TV
'Til his girth was as big as a redwood tree.

A hundred times I told him so,
To ride a horse, to play in the snow,
To ski, to golf, or poker to play,
But on that couch he just had to lay.
Domestic problems are sure to rise
In a household where boredom lies,
A wife ignored will not stay
Where life's all work and there is no play.

Some of this story I have to guess,
But the end of the tale is a hell of a mess.
We may never agree if his wife left first
As he slaked his thirst
Or stayed to see
The first drunken spree.

After the First Drunken Spree,
Alone in his house with only his son,
He's driven to drink and not for fun.
In a place unknown he becomes very drunk.

A man he meets with a pipe that stunk.
"Puff my pipe and you will see
Your troubles dissolved through eternity."

From Carter's first puff he was hooked clean.
Crack was the link to his twisted gene.
For days and nights he neither slept nor ate,
As he smoked with new friends he would normally hate.
In his unreal world he'd hide in the smoke,   ·
A barroom orator without any joke.

His wife and his kids and all his friends too
Could not conceive what they could do.
For one short time he agreed to some aid,
But the link to the coke made him afraid.
And back to the smoke that swells the brain—
Crack was to become king again.

The saga of Carter was started for fun
And now could end with a knife or a gun.
His brain has been cooked by months of smoke
And all he wants is another toke.

With all the misery that crack did cause
We can only hope that someday he'll pause
And see the light from friends he forgot,
As this is the power that will ease his lot.

So, friend of mine, listen soon—
The road you travel will lead to ruin.
The longer you travel, the further you go.
What you reap is what you sow.
Turn back now as quick as you can,
Show your friends you're still a man.

Wesley Arthur Carter had a massive heart attack in September 1994. Ami and Sam lost a great dad, I lost a great friend, and somewhere some distance up the trail, Georgia had lost a great husband.

♠ FRED ENGEBRETSON

Tom Engebretson was one of the first European pioneers to come to Anahim Lake. John Jacob Lunas and his daughter, Annie, were two others, and Tom and Annie got married and ranched at Towdystan. They had four children, Lorena, Thelma, Harold and Fred. Lorena married Tim Draney, originally from Bella Coola, and they ranched for years at Lily Lake, ten miles east of Anahim Lake. Thelma married Earl McInroy and they ran the garage and post office in the town of Anahim Lake. Harold married Alice Holte, the daughter of Andy and Hattie Holte, two more of the non-Native settlers who lived on the Dean River. Harold worked for the Dominion Telegraph Company maintaining the line for a stretch of some thirty miles. His job was to keep the trees cut back from the line and to fix any trouble he could find. The section of line he maintained was bordered to the west by Bob Stranaghan and to the east by Tom Chignell.

Chignell was known as a tremendously hard worker who would clean the small jackpine trees from the line out to the road, so the dirt road would dry out quicker. Harold, on the other hand, was usually noted for doing what was necessary. One time Harold visited us at the Cless Pocket Ranch just before an inspector was due to look at the line rights-of-way. As Harold seemed to be worried about this inspection, someone tried to reassure him by saying there had been no trouble or complaints on his part of the line and that he shouldn't have anything to worry about. "Yaw, I know," he said. "But do you know that man, Chignell, has cut down half the trees in the Chilcotin, and now I've heard he's gone and got himself a grub hoe and gone down after the roots." Someone complained to Harold about how the government was always spending more

Tom Chignell was the lineman east of Harold Engebretson's line. Stan Dowling (right) was a hard-driving man who pioneered the opening of the Anahim Lake area.

money than it had and seemed to keep raising taxes to try and catch up. "Yaw, I know," Harold said. "It is sure lucky the taxpayer is a sturdy little fellow."

Harold's brother, Fred, never married and wound up living at their parents' ranch in Towdystan all his life. The road from Anahim Lake to Williams Lake ran right past his house. Fred had a small cattle ranch and a one-man sawmill. He could make any machinery work by taking bits and pieces from a pile of wrecks he had behind his house. Mickey Dorsey had taught Fred when she worked as a schoolteacher, and she once remarked that Fred was the smartest pupil she had ever had. Mickey and her husband, Lester, were pioneer ranchers in the area. Two of their several children still ranch in the area: Dave, the oldest, and Wanda, the only girl. Wanda and her husband, Roger Williams, run a trail-riding business and guide big-game hunters.

I have had some memorable conversations with Fred Engebretson. Many people stopped by his place over the years and his astute comments took on a life of their own and became legendary. Dave Hall, who once owned Nimpo Lake Store with his wife, Sheri, told me he stopped at Fred's when he first came into the country and asked Fred if he could buy some lumber from him. Fred said, "Yaw, do you know I have been cutting lumber here at Towdystan for thirty-five years, and they still want more."

I stopped in to visit Fred quite often when I was hauling freight from Williams Lake past his place. On one occasion I mentioned how fast jet airplanes were able to go, which I thought was remarkably fast. Fred replied that they weren't really that fast, as they now had a Beaver that would go nine hundred miles an hour. When Fred made a statement like that, you couldn't tell by looking at his face whether he was sincere. He would have made an excellent

Andy Holte's wife Hattie, Tom Mathews and his brother. Andy and Hatty lived west of Anahim Lake, and Tom lived much further down the Dean River.

Fred Engebretson and Fred Linder. Linder was a heavy drinker who lived at Tatla Lake and married Betty, one of Bob Graham's daughters. Bob was the original settler at Tatla Lake.

poker player. After the government changed the official temperature scale in Canada from Fahrenheit to Celsius, someone asked Fred one winter what he thought of the new measurement. "Well, I suppose it's all right," he said. "But do you know that *Celsius* is Indian for 'cold'?"

On another occasion we were talking about the Americans being in a space race with the Russians. "I guess you have heard the Americans have landed on the moon," Fred said. "But now that they are there, they don't know what to do." One time the Department of Highways was improving the road past Fred's place and crews were dumping loads of gravel on it to raise the roadbed a few inches. Fred was taking this all in when someone stopped by and asked him what was going on. His answer was, "Do you know they are spending thousands of dollars to raise the road four inches? Don't they know the road is already 4,200 feet above sea level?"

A pair of Seventh-day Adventists stopped at Fred's to see if they could get him interested in the life hereafter. After fifteen minutes of discussion they probably didn't know who was converting who. Finally, in exasperation, one of the Adventists said, "Don't you want to believe and have everlasting life, Fred?" And he replied, "Do you mean here in Towdystan?"

I was telling Fred one day that there seemed to be way fewer mosquitoes than in earlier years. "Yaw," he said, "every time a car drives to Anahim Lake it drives over dozens of mosquitoes. Each female mosquito that gets killed would have had thousands of baby mosquitoes, so you can see why there aren't as many mosquitoes now."

Willie Sulin, the Native guide, tracker and bushman who had found Tory Jack in the wilderness, lived two miles west of Fred's place. The two men were good friends and used to kid each other a lot. On one occasion there was talk of game guides having to take a written test for their guide's licence. It wasn't long before Fred's fertile mind hatched up a story. He told Willie that the government put out a questionnaire to all game guides, and if they didn't answer all the questions right, they wouldn't get their licence. "Do you know what the first question is, Willie?" Fred asked. "It's why doesn't a cow moose have horns." Willie probably got as big a kick out of it as Fred did.

Fred inherited a small parcel of land in Bella Coola, and over the years the timber on it became quite valuable. As the price of lumber rose higher and higher, someone asked Fred why he didn't sell while prices were booming. "Well," he said, "if I don't hit this boom, then I'll hit the next one."

One day a fellow named Jack Bevin stopped at Fred's place in Towdystan, and the two of them became lifelong best friends. Jack had about everything going for him. He looked like Clark Gable and was quite a ladies' man. When he was younger he had been quite athletic and a pretty good wrestler. When I knew him he was heavy, but he was just naturally a big man. He owned a large logging outfit in Nanaimo and had a couple of Beaver airplanes. He obviously wasn't short of money.

Jack loved to hunt. Every summer he came up to Nimpo Lake in one of his Beavers and stayed in a big house on the lake that he had purchased. He and Fred spent the summer drinking and planning hunting trips while partying with local friends. Jack loved to eat and was a great cook, very finicky about his cooking. One time someone lifted the lid on some rice he was cooking and he threw it away and started over again.

Fred told me that one time they had flown a camp into the mountains, where they were going to hunt bears. Jack even had a live sheep taken in for bait. They didn't get a bear but had a good week trying. He usually brought a pilot along with his Beaver, but he himself was a very good pilot, and if he had a heavy payload or the weather was rough, he would take over the controls for take-off or landing. One time Jack organized a goose hunt on Nimpo Lake. He knew the path that the geese took at the east end of the lake. He was to do the shooting, and he had other people scare up the geese. He had taken the plug out of his shotgun and put in six shells. When the geese were flushed over him, he shot six times and got six geese.

The hunting trip to Africa that Fred and Jack took must have been quite an eye-opener for Fred. It must have been hard to believe the number of animals there were. When they took a trophy from a kill, anything they left was eaten entirely, in short order. Their guide, who was six and a half feet tall, was the toughest man Fred had ever seen. Someone had apparently crossed him once and the guide had killed him. When he told one of his assistants to do something, I guess they knew he meant it.

Fred and Jack came home from Africa by way of England. The night before they were to fly home to Canada, they went out for dinner. The head waiter took their order and told them, "The wait-ah will bring your watah." Fred said England was the only place he couldn't understand the language.

X

♠ THE BRYANT FAMILY

What attracted the first white settlers to the high altitude of the West Chilcotin is not easy to figure out. It couldn't have been the fertile soil or the length of the growing season or the mildness of the winters. It certainly wasn't the easy access to a well-built system of roads and highways. Some areas of Canada, such as the prairies, were populated by promises of rich farmland. Other areas had rushes of people with a lust for gold. This didn't happen in the far West Chilcotin or the Anahim Lake area.

A deep-rooted pioneering spirit must have driven a lot of white people to settle this area, that and a strong curiosity about the adventure to be had in a new environment by independent-thinking people who wanted a big change in their life.

The Bryants were a family that fit this pattern. Cyrus Lord Bryant and his wife, Phyllis, had moved to the Fraser River country north of Williams Lake from Montana. Along the river, almost anything they wanted to eat could be grown. Deer were plentiful and easy to hunt for a supply of meat. At times the river was full of fish. They were living in a poor man's paradise.

In the fall of 1922, Cyrus obtained a place west of the Graham Ranch at Tatla Lake. There was a small cabin on it and he had put up a little hay on the place. By now he and Phyllis had four children: Bunch was four, Alfred seven, Caroline eight and Jane nine. In December 1922, Cyrus decided to move lock, stock and barrel to the little homestead west of Tatla Lake. This trip was 150 miles by wagon road. To set out on a journey of this magnitude at this time of year, with a team and a wagon and a young family, was almost unthinkable. Winter weather is unpredictable and starts to get very serious and often downright nasty. The temperature was known to reach 70 below in those days, and snow was measured in feet. Cyrus must have been driven by the pioneering instinct that didn't allow any thought that you wouldn't accomplish what you set out to do. Centuries before, sailors thought they might sail off the edge of the world, yet they kept on sailing. Decades later, engineers thought a jet might disintegrate when going through the sound barrier but this never slowed down Chuck Yeager, the first pilot to fly faster than the speed of sound. Cyrus had this spirit and determination when he left the comfort and security of his place on the Fraser and set out for Tatla Lake.

He drove a four-horse wagon with most of the family's possessions in it. Dean Holt, a young boy of sixteen, drove a two-wheeled wagon. Phyllis drove the buckboard, and the older kids came behind on horseback, driving their six Hereford cows. On the second night out, a foot and a half of snow fell, and it collapsed their tent in the middle of the night. By the next day it had turned very cold and the horses had tough going. Whenever they came to a rancher's place along the road they were welcomed for the night, which probably explains how they were able to continue. On about the fourth day out, it turned 40 below. The wagons pulled hard through the frozen snow. The kids bringing up the cows behind the wagons had to walk almost continuously to stay warm enough to withstand the cold. Those in the wagons were not experienced enough or prepared to use the heat from the lantern, so they must have piled clothes on themselves and little Bunch in the buckboard, and suffered in silence. They would have been unable to walk as a means of warming up.

The kids fell considerably behind the wagons. When they finally caught up, long after dark, Cyrus had parked the two wagons and lit a fire. Everyone went through the painful process of warming up, then they left the two wagons for the night and Cyrus put a lantern in the big wagon, as there were freezables in it. Being covered, the wagon would hold a certain amount of heat. Everybody except the kids got into the buckboard and went on to Norman Lee's. The kids rode their horses. The Lees' ranch was about four miles away, but now they could trot right along and it didn't take long to get there.

The Lees welcomed them with the hospitality that seemed to go with the turf in the Chilcotin. The comfort and warmth of a house and a hot meal after the day they had had must have been indescribable and would have put them in the best of spirits. They would have slept the sleep of the dead.

The next morning Dean and Cyrus went back for the wagons, but they returned with only the smaller wagon. The lantern had somehow set fire to the big wagon, destroying all their winter food, spare clothing, bedding, dishes and Phyllis's prize possession, her Heintzman piano. Phyllis was an accomplished pianist and must have spent many hours lost in her music to relieve the stress of a hard life. Losing the piano must have been a terrible blow to her. But she was a strong character with four kids to raise, and she took the tragedy in her stride and prepared herself for what they would have to do next.

A telephone line ran through the country, and by now everybody along the way knew how the Bryants were progressing. The news of their fire and their loss went up and down the phone line within an hour. Food and clothes were supplied on credit by Tommy Lee, the store owner at Alexis Creek. Much other help was offered, and they were able to continue on their way.

As the days ground on, the Bryants' horses began to play out. Cyrus finally phoned ahead to Bob Graham, who sent a team and bobsleigh for them to Knolls' ranch at Chilanko Forks. With the fresh team and a day's rest, they started the last thirty miles to Tatla Lake. The snow was deep and drifted, and the thermometer dropped to 40 below again. For three kids keeping six tired cows moving after the sleigh and cutter, this leg of the journey must have been agonizing. One would ride and two would walk in an attempt to warm up, and they would keep changing. They finally caught up to Cyrus, who had pitched the old tent and had a fire going. It was long after dark once again. The next day they made it to the Grahams' after supper, and Phyllis insisted that they continue to the homestead Cyrus had prepared. At two o'clock in the morning, on December 23, 1922, they arrived.

Travelling in those conditions, the Bryants must have gotten a little testy with each other at times. After twenty-three days on the road they also must have had great respect and admiration for each other for accomplishing such a difficult task. It is amazing that Alfred, Caroline and Jane lasted through this ordeal. They had to be three very tough and devoted kids. The only thing they did not have to endure on the trip was traffic.

The Bryants stayed on their Tatla Lake property for ten years. The kids were able to get some schooling, and Jane went to college and became a very well-known nurse. Cyrus and Phyllis made a little money working, and Alfred made a little money trapping, but they just couldn't improve their property into a cattle ranch. For a while they became friends with a guy by the name of Harold Valleau, who lived south of them in the West Branch Valley. Valleau had a reputation for being a mean, unpredictable, evil sort of person. He had split more than one head with a pistol barrel. At one point he and Cyrus got into a heated argument and Valleau reached down from his saddle horse and hit Cyrus over the head with the heavy end of his quirt. Cyrus, who was on foot, tried to pull Valleau off his horse and received several more blows. When Alfred found out about this he vowed to kill Valleau, but the opportunity never arose.

One day Lester Dorsey stopped by driving some steers to market in Williams Lake, and the Bryants got a verbal introduction to Anahim Lake. Apparently Lester had seen enough of the Bryant place to know it would never turn into anything. A month later another person, Bert Lehman, rode into their place from the west. He had a very loud voice and a much louder laugh that he just couldn't control. He invited himself to stay and proved to be very strong, a man who worked on the run. He and Alfred cut enough wood for the winter. Bert would periodically let out a yell and then let his loud laugh go. He also advertised Anahim Lake as the place the Bryants should be. Alfred was seventeen years old now. After living in a hopeless place in absolute poverty for ten years, he knew he would have to initiate the move, though his dad's iron will would be very hard to overcome. Eventually he talked his family into moving to Anahim.

On July 10, 1931, Caroline, Bunch and Alfred loaded up all

their ranching gear, put old tires on the cast-iron mower wheels so they could move it with a team, and headed out for Anahim Lake. Phyllis was living in Williams Lake by that time and Jane was at nursing school in Kamloops. By this time Caroline was eighteen, old enough to pre-empt a homestead in her own name on Corkscrew Creek, just east of Anahim Lake. Many years later she sold it to Tommy Holte, who later sold it to me.

Alfred, Bert and the girls built a comfortable log cabin at Corkscrew Creek, got some corrals built and put up some hay. It was a good-sized cabin, about eighteen by twenty-four feet on the inside, with a split-log puncheon roof covered with hay and dirt. It was typical of the rustic log cabins built in that country during those days, with a single window and a homemade door. Bert helped Alfred finish the cabin while Caroline and Bunch went back down to

When Tommy Holte was a boy, he and his two sisters, Illa and Alice, looked after several hundred sheep at their home in Lessard Lake, west of Anahim. They named most of the sheep. Sadly, the feed was not nutritious enough and most of the sheep died. Here is Tommy, later in life, bottle-feeding a wee lamb.

Tatla Lake to help Cyrus clean up their old homestead and bring everything they owned up to Anahim Lake. By this time it was late fall.

By way of moccasin telegraph, Alfred learned that Cyrus and the girls were on their way, and that Cyrus's horses were in poor shape trying to haul a very heavy load. Bert stayed to watch Alfred's place while Alfred took a saddle horse and team to meet Cyrus and the girls. The weather turned very cold as he rode the thirty-five miles before meeting Cyrus, whose horses were pretty well played out. They made it another five miles toward Anahim before camping for the night. The next night they reached Andy Holte's place at Towdystan. As Andy was short of hay, they couldn't lay over to feed their horses, so they took off the next morning with the thermometer reading 58 below zero. They travelled as far as they could in the freezing weather, then built a fire and warmed up. They repeated this a couple more times, and as the horses got more tired they travelled more and more slowly. Bert Lehman's cabin was two miles off the road, and it was decided that Alfred and Caroline would ride to it and get a fire going while Bunch and Cyrus came behind, making as good time as they could.

Alfred and Caroline had to break trail through a couple of feet of snow, which was very slow going and hard on the horses. In temperatures of 60 below it is also hard on the riders. When they finally reached the cabin, Alfred and Caroline stumbled off their horses and staggered through the snow to the door. It was all Alfred could do to lift the latch so they could get inside. As was the custom in this country during the winter, shavings, kindling and matches had been left beside the stove. With his mitts frozen to his hands, Alfred loaded the stove for lighting. Now he had to get his frozen mitts off to light a match. With no feeling in his hands, he made three clumsy attempts to get a match going. Had he not known his dad and sisters had to have warmth, he might have given up. Somehow he was able to get one match lit and get the fire going. As he and Caroline started to thaw out, Cyrus and Bunch pulled up to the cabin. They had to be helped in, as neither could walk without support. Later they learned it had dropped to 70 below that night.

Alfred later moved east of Anahim Lake to a place he called Tallywacker. That is where he met Gordon Wilson, a sixteen-year-old who had changed homes enough that he got on his horse one day at Clinton and struck out across country. He had a bedroll and enough grub to keep him alive if he missed a ranch house on his way. That and Chilcotin hospitality tided him over until he got to Anahim Lake. He was in bad need of a job and a place to stay, and who should he run into but Alfred Bryant.

Alfred gave him a job with little pay but a roof over his head and three meals a day. This was a good arrangement for both of them. Alfred needed the help at Tallywacker. The ranch provided easy access into the Ilgachuz and Itcha mountains. Alfred guided moose hunters, and he and Gordon made the hunting accessible by using Alfred's big steel-wheeled wagon. Alfred had married Caroline Harrington and they had two boys and two girls, Zeke, Cy, Rayma and Carla, and Gordon became part of the family.

Gordon told me that Alfred had little patience with animals. When he was working with them, they had to do what he wanted them to do and be quick about it. Alfred had the milk cow trained so that when he yelled at her, she would stop wherever she happened to be in the corral and put her left hind foot back in preparation for milking.

♠

One day in the 1930s, after Alfred had persuaded Rich Hobson and Pan Phillips to move to Corkscrew Creek, he decided to go hunting moose. There had been no reports of moose sign in the lower country, so he headed for the Ilgachuz Mountains with the necessary packhorses as well as Rich, Pan, Shorty King and Bert Lehman. The first night they camped in the foothills of the mountains, where there was good horse feed. By noon the next day they had climbed higher, and Alfred told the rest of them to make camp while he scouted ahead. Alfred got a moose that afternoon. The next morning he took Rich with him, and Rich shot his first moose.

They went back down the mountain with all the meat they could pack, a group of very happy hunters.

A few years earlier there had been no moose in the Anahim Lake country, only caribou. Forty miles east of Anahim Lake on Highway 20, a brush flat supported so many caribou it got the lasting name Caribou Flats. When the moose migration started, the moose came through the Ilgachuz Mountains to Anahim Lake, west to the Precipice country and south and east to Kleena Kleene. Everybody in the country lived on moose meat. There were literally hundreds of moose around. On the Cless Pocket Ranch one day when I was working in the shop, I counted sixteen moose walking across the meadow not far from the house. Moose hung around the lowlands in the winter and went into the mountains in the spring and summer.

For years Thomas Squinas had been hired to keep the wolves in check, and he had done a remarkable job of it. But after he stopped looking after the wolves, they started multiplying with the moose. They became more and more abundant and began killing livestock as well as game. This was lucky for the moose. At that time, strychnine was easy to get. I knew of several ranchers across the country who took it upon themselves to keep the numbers down by poisoning wolves.

Alfred Bryant went to Vancouver to help Rich and Pan get their immigration papers and the supplies they would be needing. It was his first trip there, and also his first elevator ride. He was able to wrestle his suitcase away from the bellboy when he tried to carry it to Alfred's room. With Alfred's help, Rich and Pan were able to pick up some horses on their way back to the Chilcotin, and from there they rode into history.

Alfred Bryant and Bert Lehman stayed close and became lifelong friends. Bert was a very outgoing and jolly fellow, and loud. When he laughed he could make your ears ring. He was also known for his strength. At a party one night when some of the men were showing off their physical abilities, it was decided that Stanley Dowling should put a wrestling hold on Bert and see if he could get out of it. Stanley had a reputation for being a very tough fighter, in

Anahim Winter Trail

written in winter of 1939/40 by Alfred Bryant
July 16, 1915 - June 6, 1988

The rider sits hunched in his saddle, the temperature's dropping fast.
With his collar turned up, his ear-flaps down, he faces the icy blast.

The trees are faintly visible, through the swirling, drifting snow.
The two miles might as well be ten, for his cayuse is tired and slow.

As his horse ploughs wearily homeward, through snow that is up to his chest,
He staggers, a bit, off the drifted trail, and his rider pulls him up, for a rest.
Oh, just to roll a cigarette and to draw the smoke in deep;
A pot of coffee, a good warm house, supper, rest, and sleep.

He has dodged most snow-laden branches that came his way through the day,
But some snow dropped in the saddle, it melted and froze that way.

The seat of his saddle is icy, though he cleared out most with his hand.
His pants are stiff and frozen. What a god-forsaken land!

Now, to add to his misery, darkness is falling fast.
His mittens are frozen upon his hands, he hopes that his horse can last.

His feet feel numb and lifeless, he's afraid they're frozen some.
He'd like to get off and walk, a bit, but knows it cannot be done.

For a man can't walk in snow that deep, even for just a while.
Floundering through that drifted snow, he couldn't go half a mile.

He wriggles his toes, in his moccasins, while his horse plods bravely ahead.
He'd feel just as cold, if he did get off, with his feet so lifeless and dead.

He tries to divert his mind from the cold to things that are warm and bright.
He thinks of his wife cooking supper. Thank God! Now there's the light!

His numb hands fumble the cinch-hook, he turns his horse to the hay.
He stumbles blindly into the house, thanking God its the end of that day.

boxing and street fighting. He wasn't tall but he was heavy-set and a hard worker, and pretty strong. Stanley put the hold on Bert, and when Bert got the nod to see if he could break the hold, he threw Stanley across the room. Stanley later said he didn't think anyone could get out of that hold. Luckily Bert had no yen for fighting. I never heard of him getting into a fight.

In 1938, Alfred and Bert built the first bridge across the Dean River, next to where the Anahim Lake Stampede Grounds are today. I remember hearing stories of them manhandling some of the big stringer logs the bridge deck was built on. Alfred was no ninety-seven-pound weakling either. It's a wonder they never hurt themselves.

Years ago people provided their own entertainment. They did this by pulling tricks on someone, beating someone in a trade or arguing about current events. One day at Cless Pocket Ranch, my grandfather, Adolph Christensen, decided his lighter was about to pack it in, so he fixed it up so it would work all right. Bert Lehman happened to come in for a cup of coffee, and as soon as he had time to settle into his coffee, Adolph made a pitch about how good his lighter was. He asked Bert if he was interested in making a trade. Bert let out a very loud "wha, ha, ha" and told Adolph that he would like to trade him but his lighter had quit working on him.

Adolph looked Bert's lighter over and could see it was a good lighter that just needed a part or two. He put in a flint, a piece of wick and some lighter fluid, and the lighter worked perfectly.

Adolph then showed Bert his own lighter, expounding on its virtues and pointing out what a good make of lighter it was. He said he really didn't want to trade his lighter off but thought Bert could use a better lighter, and would trade him straight across. Bert yelled out that his lighter worked so good now that he would just keep it. "Wha, ha, ha!"

Not to be outdone, Adolph got some rubber doughnuts that looked like the real McCoy but were horrible to bite into and impossible to chew. The next time Bert happened by, Adolph was ready. He had a couple of cups of coffee poured when Bert came through the door, and one doughnut laid out on a little plate.

It looked pretty delicious. A bachelor in Anahim Lake wouldn't see a doughnut or a cookie for months at a time. As soon as Bert came through the door, he let out a yell about Adolph saving him the last doughnut and grabbed it and shoved it in his mouth as if he was going to eat it in one bite. I was a very young lad at this time and my grandfather had briefed me on what to look forward to. Adolph and I had a great laugh over the whole thing. Bert yelled, "That doughnut was sure tough and Adolph must have cooked it. Wha, ha, ha!"

One day when Bert was at the Cless Pocket Ranch, he and Billy Dagg and Adolph got into a fierce argument over something that had once been legal but was no longer allowed. Bert had been arguing that it was still allowed but as he could see he was losing the argument, he yelled out, "Well, you usta could! Wha, ha, ha!" This saying was used around the ranch for months afterward.

Alfred, Cyrus, Bunch and Caroline kept improving their little place on Corkscrew Creek. A small shop, a chicken coop and corrals were built. They made their table, chairs and benches by axe from logs on their place. Their mattresses were sacks filled with hay, laid on homemade bunks. The Bryants got their groceries from my dad's little store on the Cless Pocket Ranch. They bought what they needed on jawbone and paid when Alfred caught a little fur or found some work. Sometimes Alfred would take a string of six or eight packhorses to the end of the road in Bella Coola for a pre-arranged load of staples the Bryants needed. Andy would phone the order to his dad, Adolph, at his store in Bella Coola. Adolph would carefully weigh each pack for the horses and haul them up the road by vehicle to meet Alfred. Payment was always made in the same manner, by jawbone.

One fall Alfred got on a beef drive through Bob French, who wanted to join the bigger drive from Anahim Lake. Ed Collet was the trail boss. Alfred, Jimmy Sulin and Ed's ranching partner, Tim Draney, were the cowboys. On their way through Arthur Knoll's ranch at Puntzi, they picked up more cattle and another rider, Billy Dagg, who later became my dad's foreman on the Cless Pocket

L to R: Ronald Waite, Tommy Holte, Tim Draney, Andy Christensen, Ed Collet and me, at seven years old.

Ranch and taught me lots of things. A cowboy and saddle horse were paid a dollar and a half a day, and beef prices were no better. Alfred got back with the promise of a cow and calf and a yearling heifer to be delivered the next year.

Caroline and Bunch joined Phyllis in Williams Lake, which gave them the chance to become more sophisticated. Jane was in Kamloops, training to become a nurse. The Bryants expanded their hay operation by getting a little hay lease west of the Lake Meadows at Cless Pocket. We always called it Bryant Camp. Eventually the girls got married, and Alfred and Cyrus got a place they called the Tallywacker, twelve miles or so east of Anahim Lake, where they guided for moose and raised cattle.

Some cowboys walk with a roll from one foot to the other, whether to hear their spurs jingle or just because they picked it up from long years in the saddle is anyone's guess. A young cowboy named Ronald Waite, fresh over from England and just starting out cowboying, was doing the above described walk at a community roundup. As he passed by Jim Holt, an old seasoned cowboy who came from Texas,

Jim drawled, "Look at that Englishman, he walks like a half-grown mallard duck." Ronald Waite married Caroline Bryant.

Jane Lehman (no relation to Bert Lehman) became a registered nurse and worked for the local Natives and anyone else who required her medical attention. All trips to administer to the sick or hurt were made on horseback, regardless of the weather. Jane would accept no praise or special recognition for her services. She was awarded the Red Cross Florence Nightingale Medal posthumously—a fitting honour for a deserving lady.

The third Bryant sister, Bunch Trudeau, lived in the Batnuni country northeast of Anahim Lake. Alfred Bryant retired to Bella Coola after years of guiding and ranching east of Anahim.

♠ ALEX FRASER

Alex Fraser was one of BC's best-liked politicians of all time. His yen for public life may have been seeded in his youth. Alex's father,

Alex Fraser rides toy airplane at the opening of Anahim Lake airport.
DON & MARILYN BAXTER COLLECTION.

Purchasing pricey white-bellied lynx skins from Lashaway Alec in Quesnel. Though Lashaway lived in a very remote area, Alex Fraser visited him on one of his campaigns. PHOTO KRIS ANDREWS.

John Fraser, was MLA for the Cariboo constituency from 1912 to 1916, and MP for the federal Cariboo riding from 1925 to 1935. Alex started in public office when he was elected mayor of Quesnel. He held this position for twenty years, an almost unheard-of length of time for a mayor to last. He was elected as MLA for the Cariboo in 1969 and held this position until his death in 1989. He was minister of highways from 1975 to 1987.

Before entering politics, Alex and a partner had a freight line that ran between Vancouver and Quesnel. In the winter of 1945, the Canadian military conducted manoeuvres between Bella Coola and Anahim Lake called the Polar Bear Expedition. This project consisted of a thousand men with a range of machinery, including ski planes, bulldozers equipped to operate in the snow and 120 horses. At this time Alex was a staff sergeant stationed in Williams Lake. One of his responsibilities was to have proper feed flown in for the horses.

When Alex decided to run for MLA in 1969 to represent the

Cariboo Chilcotin, he had already established his presence in the region by travelling from one end of his riding to the other. He met and talked to anyone he could get to. Once he talked to someone, he knew a lot about them, and with his phenomenal memory for names he never forgot them. Once when talking to Alex I mentioned flying into a Native trapper's place on a river thirty miles west of Quesnel, out in the wilderness. I said the trapper's name was Lashaway Alec, and Alex said he knew Lashaway and had once visited his house to meet him and solicit his vote.

Alex Fraser never left a stone unturned. He never missed a major event or public gathering in any of the communities in his riding. Someone told me that he and his wife, Gertrude, used to quiz each other on people's names in different families and different communities—an excellent way to refresh their memories on names and happenings.

When Alex was elected in 1969, he knew from his travels what needed to be done for the people in every area of his riding. Sometimes he ran ahead of his constituents in his thinking, and he was known to get roads built so fast that a couple of ranchers

Don Baxter presents Alex with a beaver skin. Don and his wife Marilyn owned the other store in Anahim Lake. DON & MARILYN BAXTER COLLECTION.

Alex cuts the ribbon at the new airport. The airport and hydro were two main innovations that Don Baxter and I had pushed for.

DON & MARILYN BAXTER COLLECTION.

complained they would lose their solitude. In between elections Alex maintained communication with people in his riding. He was known as a man who kept his promises and got things done.

As highways minister from 1975 to 1987, Alex got so much of the road rebuilt between Williams Lake and Bella Coola that it could rightly have been called the Alex Fraser Highway. He became so well known and so highly thought of that someone commented he would be the least likely to lose an election held anywhere in Canada.

Any politician knows that the lion's share of the privileges gained by the victor in an election must be shared with those who got him elected, or might get him elected again. The Social Credit party did big projects with this in mind. I told Alex I wondered about the provincial government getting into the coal-mining business at Tumbler Ridge. Japan was to get most of the coal, and it wasn't long before they bought a coal outlet in Australia as well. Alex's reason was that the Social Credit party needed the northern vote. That made sense to me. I knew without a doubt that I got the liquor store licence in Anahim Lake because I was a big backer of Alex and his party.

I attended one of Alex's victory parties in Williams Lake. After formal greetings and hand shaking, Alex announced his plans for our riding. He was in his glory in that room, being at the pinnacle of power. Nobody would dare interfere with his chain of thought. He knew what had to be done and would see that it was done.

The thought of having a modern sawmill and high-scale logging in Anahim Lake scared a good number of West Chilcotin inhabitants into trying to block the operation. One method used was fire. At one time there were as many people setting fires as putting them out. This was a dangerous situation. Fire burns indiscriminately. On a trip to Williams Lake I ran into Alex and told him what was going on. He blew his stack at the thought of people getting away with civil disobedience, and said the mill would go ahead come hell or high water. It did, at the additional cost of a million or two for firefighting.

In 1986 the Social Credit Party chose a new leader, Bill Vander Zalm, who was not a friend of Alex Fraser. By this time Alex had had his larynx removed because of throat cancer. The 1986 provincial election campaign was Alex's last one, and with Gertrude's help he won by a landslide, even though he was unable to talk. That year the Cariboo riding had been reorganized to be represented by two MLAs, and Neil Vant, also representing the Social Credit Party, slid into the other Cariboo seat on the momentum of Alex's great popularity. Vander Zalm then gave Alex's old job as highways minister to Vant, and Alex openly fought Vander Zalm over the privatization of the highways ministry. He kept it up until his death in the spring of 1989.

In the September 1989 by-election after Alex's death, David Zirnhelt won the vacant Cariboo seat for the New Democratic Party. Before his death Alex had predicted Zirnhelt would succeed him, and Gertrude Fraser publicly endorsed Zirnhelt's campaign.

Alex Fraser fought for what he thought was right, until the day he died. One tribute that was not paid to him in public was that he was one tough son of a bitch.

When watching Connie's slow amble, people rarely guessed that he was an extremely good athlete. He played hockey and semi-professional baseball.

FAY BUCHANAN COLLECTION.

♠ CONNIE KING

Connie King was a famous professional hockey player who used to spend his summers working on the Cless Pocket Ranch. He drove a horse mower most of the time. When he quit playing hockey, he obtained a small ranch southwest of Anahim Lake. One spring while looking after his cattle that were in the process of calving, he was attacked by a grizzly bear. He had one eye bitten out and many other lacerations. He spent a long time getting patched up in a hospital in Vancouver. Eventually he was able to come back to Anahim Lake, and he seemed to be the same Connie, less one eye. One day I was talking to Connie when a pickup with huge oversized tires drove by. The wheels elevated the vehicle two or three feet in the air. Connie said, "You know, that driver must have one testicle the size of a timothy seed, and the other must be just a little bitty one."

♠ MADDIE JACK

In 1963 Maddie Jack, a Native lady from Ulkatcho, was working with her husband, John, on the Mud Lake Ranch about twelve miles southeast of Anahim Lake. Some horses had strayed so they took two saddle horses and rode in different directions to try and find them. Maddie came upon some very thick jackpine that her horse couldn't go into, so she tied up the horse to a tree and continued the search on foot. She had walked about a mile when she ran into a sow grizzly bear and two cubs. She had always been told that if you stayed still, a grizzly would leave you alone. The mother bear walked around behind her, bit her in the neck and then threw her to the ground. Then it bit her all over the back and legs and picked her up and shook her. Maddie lost consciousness, and when she came to, she was covered up with dirt and mud. She managed to free herself and walked back to her horse. By that time her husband was there, and she was so covered in dirt and blood that John hardly recognized her. Maddie spent the rest of the summer in hospital and ended up with something like two hundred stitches. Over the next four years she returned to the hospital several times for more treatments. I don't know of any other person who was chewed up, mauled and buried by a grizzly who lived to tell the story.

♠ BEAR

One summer at Behind Meadow, two miles west of the ranch headquarters, I was designated to shoot a deer for meat to feed the haying crew. I took the only gun in camp, an old 30-30. I later found out the gun wasn't sighted in—I couldn't have hit a barrel with it if I had been inside the barrel. I rode a horse up the slope of the Illgatcho Mountains behind the haying camp, and when I came upon a lot of deer sign, I tied up my horse and hunted on foot. I shot at and missed a deer I should have killed. On my way back to my horse I crested a hill and came upon a black bear eating berries at the bottom of the hill. As the bear was very close and hadn't seen me, I decided to shoot it in the head or miss it entirely so I wouldn't wound it. The bear was busy eating berries, unaware of my presence, when I pulled the trigger. At the sound of the rifle, the bear exploded into action, charging up the hill I was on, then instantly disappearing from my view because of the bulge of the hill. I took off down the side of the hill, flying low. The bear and I passed each other just feet apart. I shot at him from the hip in full stride and continued on to my horse and back to camp. That bear and I both got a pretty good scare.

♠ BOB DRANEY

Bob Draney was one of the sons of Tom Draney, who built the fish cannery on the coast with my grandfather, John Clayton. Bob worked for years on the Cless Pocket Ranch during my time there. One of his favourite expressions when someone was in a hurry or acted nervous was, "He's like fart in a mitt, looking for a thumb

Well-known men in the area: (L to R) Tommy Elkins, Bob Draney, Doug Norberg, Bob Smith and Raphael Alphonse.

Bob Draney and Ken Stranaghan on one of our Itcha Mountain safaris.

hole." Bob developed a bad case of piles working on the ranch. His work required riding horses, driving horse-drawn equipment and lifting heavy items, so the piles demanded a lot of his attention. He finally got the opportunity to go to Bella Coola for an operation. When the doctor came to see him after the operation, and asked him how he felt, Bob said, "Oh, I feel like there is two tom cats up my ass having a stake race." Bob made a complete recovery, and when I saw him and his wife, June, when he was eighty-seven, he didn't look any older than he did twenty years before.

♠ BOB COHEN

Bob Cohen was very good at handling and working with horses, so he was often hired to do guiding jobs and to look after cattle. As a group of us ranchers around Anahim Lake were permitted to run cattle in the Itcha Mountains, we provided Bob with a cabin in a strategic location for shelter and got him to look after the cattle for us. He was a very capable man who didn't want anyone to do his thinking for him, and he was happy to be left on his own in charge of the cattle for the summer. One thing Bob had never been

Bob Cohen looks like I paid him too much for his fur. Foiled again.

accused of was using too much water to wash his hands and face and dishes. One fall when we journeyed to the Itchas to round up the herd and bring it back to Anahim Lake, Tommy Holte, one of the ranchers, complained of an upset stomach and a bout of diarrhea. When we got to the cabin for the night, a quick look around indicated that the dishes and pots and pans could use a good scouring before being used by us ordinary souls. We got the biggest container available and soaked everything in lots of soap and boiling water. After an hour or two of this treatment, everything was scraped off and scrubbed down until things looked pretty shiny. The wash pail was left on the table. The next morning Tommy came into the cabin from saddling his horse, still feeling bad, so he grabbed a dipper, filled it from the pail and downed a good helping of dishwater. "Chrish," Tommy said. "What kind of water was that? It sure tasted awful." A couple hours later as we were rounding up the cattle, Tommy said, "Chrish, I don't know what was in that water, but it sure cured the shits." I guess the end justifies the means.

Steep rocky ground in the Itcha Mountains. Great caution was taken to ensure none of the horses were injured.

♠ LOCAL LANDSCAPE

As kids growing up in Bella Coola, we spent a lot of our time on the tide flats west of town. Over the centuries the Bella Coola River had formed an estuary with the Pacific Ocean, from one side of the valley to the other. It was evident that the sand in the flats was brought down from the upper valley by the river. When the tide was in, the sand was covered by the ocean, thus the name tide flats. The mountains in Bella Coola are very steep and mostly granite. Living in this valley I would often hear small rockslides coming off the steep slopes. On riding horseback up the Atnarko River on our way to Anahim Lake, we would pass by huge rockslides that were not very steep. Once in a while a rock could be heard to move a foot or two. As we rode along the Atnarko River for miles on these trips, it was easy to see that all the rocks would eventually wind up in the river and then as sand in the tide flats at Bella Coola. This process was going to take a while.

The geology of the earth is fascinating. Erosion eventually breaks up all earth above sea level, and rivers carry this matter into oceans, where it is piled up so thick and heavy it sinks under the earth's crust and forces mountains upward. That is why the Rocky Mountains are full of shellfish remains. Geological time is measured in millions of years, planetary time in billions of years. In those terms, any life on earth lasts for the blink of an eye. Astronomers are seeing out into space at least twelve billion light years with the latest telescopes, and Earth is estimated to be four and a half billion years old. In the 1600s the accepted age of the Earth was six thousand years.

I was watching a prominent federal Conservative politician being interviewed on television one night not long ago, and when he got around to saying how old the earth was, he said, "somewhere between five and six thousand years old." He added that people lived with dinosaurs at that time. I couldn't believe what I was hearing. He must not have read a scientific book in his life, and he must wear welding goggles when he goes outside. I fully expected that in his next breath he was going to say the earth was flat. I wasn't the only one who heard him, and the joke soon circulated that this fellow thought *The Flintstones* was a documentary.

LIFE IS A GAMBLE

AFTER THE WILLIAMS LAKE POKER GAMES BROKE UP, I STARTED going to Vegas and playing casino poker. This was a different poker than I was used to, and I read some books on the subject. In "hold 'em," the main game, each player is dealt two cards. There is a betting round, then the dealer flops three common cards up, then there is another betting round. The next card up is called the turn, and the final card is called the river. Both of these rounds are bet on. The best five cards to make a poker hand wins.

Tournament poker started becoming very popular at about that time, and it was pretty exciting. Tournaments were hard to win but paid good money to the top three winners. I played tournaments in western Canada, Reno, Vegas and Pendleton, Oregon. In 2009 I was playing in one of Vern Ashley's tournaments at his pool hall in Williams Lake when a young player came up to me and showed me a complete record of all my live tournaments from 2001 to 2008, which he had downloaded from the internet. I had grossed $140,601. After tournament entry fees, travel expenses, hotel rooms, meals and so on, I estimate a net gain of about $14,000. A hard way to make an easy living.

When you play poker for hours at a time, you can encounter many frustrations. You can have a good legitimate hand and play it properly and still get beaten by someone who catches a lucky card to a ridiculous draw. This is called getting "donkeyed." You have to force yourself to hold back a tirade of swearing and abuse, and pretend you like it. Over the years of playing poker with hundreds of different players of many nationalities, the best-mannered people I have ever played with are the Native Indians. They get the gold medal for manners (this, of course, is *sans vino*).

Sometimes I travelled around to poker games with my son, Chuck, or my daughter Andrea. Occasionally, when other things didn't interfere, the three of us have gone together. This is a special thrill. Not many poker players on the circuit have three members of the family in the same tournament.

Around 2002, I started playing online party poker on the computer. I won two $20 satellites into two $225 buy-in tournaments. Each of them had about a thousand players in it. I won both of them for over $100,000 total. This wouldn't happen again if I played for over a thousand years.

Andrea and I played in another tournament and won a ship cruise out of San Diego, with a $10,000 entry in a tournament on the ship. I took Kris and Chuck with me. I was assigned a table that Chip Chet was on. Both Chip and his wife are professional players, and Chip had such a run of cards that you couldn't beat him with a club. It wasn't too long before I was knocked out of the tournament, but we did get to see the sights in San Diego.

The cruise was just another benefit from poker. When we were told how much fuel the ship used per day, we all thought it should have been anchored at sea. I had left $20,000 of my online winnings in my account and thought of it as a licence to print money. In two or three months my online account was broke, and I haven't played on this account since.

Years ago the government in Costa Rica decided to promote poker in their country. I was one of the lucky ones who received an offer of an all-expense-paid trip to the capital of Costa Rica, in 1990, for a tournament of several days. The flight, the hotel, the food and all the ground transportation was paid for. On first entering the room where the poker tournament was to be held, I was dumbfounded by the number of beautiful women who were attending

Andrea and me getting ready to downhill ski in Jasper.

the poker tables. Most of the players seemed to have cameras, and before the tournament started they took pictures of the girls. Two of them, beautiful redheaded twins, were photographed dozens of times. It was like Oscar night in Hollywood. I later learned that these young ladies were working their way through college. When I went out and explored the town, the people provided hospitality that I had never seen or even dreamed of. One morning I got up late and found that the hotel café was closed. As I walked out the door, one of the workers called me back in and arranged for me to have breakfast. All they would take for this was a tip. When it was time for me to leave, I realized this had been as close to heaven as I was likely to get. That was the only time the event was held. I learned later that someone had absconded with the funds they were using to promote it.

In the early days of poker, smoking was quite fashionable. I had smoked as a teenager in Bella Coola, but the combination of cigarettes and damp, cold winter days had an adverse effect on my tonsils, and I quit smoking a couple of times because of a very sore throat. Later on, when I lived in the Interior, poker players saw nothing wrong with smoking. To sit with people who smoked was terribly aggravating. Sometimes the second-hand smoke gave me a headache, and as the game went on it felt like my eyes were on fire. In this environment I started smoking again so I could tolerate everyone else's smoke. Finally smoking fell out of fashion at the games, and it has been banned from all places I have played. The last time I quit smoking I used snuff as a pacifier, and when I finally lost the desire to smoke, I gave up the snuff. This was not an easy chore. I still can't tolerate second-hand smoke, and I don't envy people who smoke. It is said to be one of the hardest drugs to stop using. It is also said to kill half the people who use it.

♠

Running a store is another kind of gamble, whether or not you play double or nothing with your customers. During my thirty-five year tenure as owner of A.C. Christensen Ltd., I had more than my share of break-ins and robberies. A judge and his retinue would come to

Anahim Lake every couple of months or so, to try and sort out the misdemeanours, such as the odd hard-working, heavy-drinking paleface who would have one cup too many and get charged with assault, or a late-night visit to the store when supplies got low at a party on the reserve.

The store was bugged for sound to my house a couple of hundred feet away. This made robbery very difficult. Once when I heard two or three people trying to get into the store, I went up there with a 30-30 rifle and accosted one of the intruders. The light was poor and I couldn't recognize him, but the gun was loaded and cocked and we had a very dangerous standoff. He wisely took off, as did the others. These would-be robbers were good guys doing a foolish and dangerous thing. I never carried a gun after that.

One night I caught a robber who had sprung the bottom of the warehouse door, and then got stuck half in and half out of the warehouse. The work I did on his stomach soon revealed his identity to me—another good guy doing something he shouldn't be doing. That night my son-in-law, Jim Redpath, was staying with me, but in my haste to stop the robbery I hadn't asked him for assistance. This was probably lucky, as he was way handier in this kind of situation than I was.

One night I heard someone trying to get into the store past the fan we had installed to get fresh air into the building. When I looked out the window, I saw him silhouetted by the outside lights on the store. My heart started to race. I phoned the local police and a man came over with his siren blaring. He caught the intruder, another good guy, but this one wound up with the wrong judge and did time.

Not all robbers are good guys. We also had slimeballs who would case the place and then gain entry by smashing a window. They would do more damage than a rogue elephant. One night they robbed my house in this manner and then robbed a trailer down the street from the store. They smashed a collection of porcelain dolls in the trailer, and the woman living there with her husband was having enough trouble without that.

By the mid-1980s, most people were learning how the Natives had been treated in their first encounters with the Europeans 150 years ago. They were cheated, robbed and lied to. Every agreement they made with the Europeans was broken. Maybe the main judge in the area read the history, because local thieves called him the catch-and-release judge. A Caucasian victim of crime got the same consideration as the mouse droppings that were swept out of the courtroom after the session was over. Chuck and I decided to build living quarters onto the store, and that was the end of slimeball thieves and the court system for me.

♠

Sometimes there were small troubles within the store, and when a clerk should have rectified a situation, I would leave a note for that person. I saved two of these notes under the heading "The two poo poos of July."

Number One: Female employee was observed throwing out a quantity of milk. Reason given: the milk was too cold. It is believed this lady runs on two switches. Both apparently had been accidentally thrown.

Number Two: A robbery had taken place in the store. Two loads of stolen goods were being brought back. Broken bottles and dented, flattened beer cans littered the warehouse floor. The thief was loading up with clothes and makeup in front of clerk. Female employee was noted not to have strayed far from two mike boxes used to sit on. It is believed she may have been suffering from complete paralysis, been in a coma, or had just received a pre-frontal lobotomy operation. It was duly noted that neither case contributed to the profitability of the store.

♠

By the 1980s the fur market had become yet another gamble, after many ups and downs since the Hudson's Bay Company started buying fur several centuries ago. I had hit fifteen years of boom time in the business, but now the market was changing dramatically. Animal-rights activists were raising big trouble for people who wore furs, going as far as throwing paint on some ladies' coats. Sensational photos of leg-hold traps were shown as barbarous ways of catching fur-bearing animals.

Another social change was taking place for the Natives who lived out in the wilderness. In the late 1970s the federal government decreed that children had to be educated and families had to move to where schools were located. This was very hard on older family members, and some of them wound up in town with nothing to do. After being self-sufficient for eons, their tie to nature had been cut and now they were solely supported by welfare. Some damned fine people had the rug pulled from under them, and a generation of trappers was pretty well wiped out.

By about 1989 the fur market had collapsed. At its height, a good lynx skin could bring a thousand dollars. That is when I bought a new Citabria airplane for fifteen thousand dollars, or fifteen lynx skins. Then the price of a lynx skin dropped to a hundred dollars and a new bush plane cost about fifty thousand dollars, or five hundred lynx skins.

Many fewer people were living in the bush, and lodge owners had their own planes, so I sold my last Bellanca Scout. Then Chuck and I decided to sell the store. He worked in Williams Lake as a carpenter, and I wanted easier access to outside poker games. Besides that, I was no longer thirty-nine. In 1999, Andrea came back from Alberta and helped me in the store. In 2000, Al Elsey, a former realtor in Williams Lake who I had known for many years, hooked me up with a second cousin of mine whom I had never met. This fellow's name was Norm McLean. He and his wife, Mona, and two sons, John and David, lived in Vancouver, where Norm was a lumber broker and Mona taught school. John ran a Canadian Tire store. He had been working for a fishing lodge on the coast one summer when one of the clients he was looking after complained about everything John did for him. He was downright miserable to John, and when the party was getting ready to fly out, this fellow asked John to go to the cookhouse and get him a sandwich that he could eat on the plane. John went and got the sandwich and gave it to the guy, who immediately complained that there was something in it he didn't like. John opened the sandwich and ground it in the fellow's face. This guy was high up in the Canadian Tire organization and hired John on the spot.

The McLeans came to our store in Anahim Lake, liked what they saw and bought it. They also bought a cabin on the lake, and Norm and Mona still reside there when they help the boys run the store. When we sold the store, it had been in the Christensen name for 102 years.

♠

There are some gambles a businessman should not take, and doing without insurance is one of them. I would have been in dire financial straits more than once if I had not carried a considerable amount of insurance on everything of value that I owned. The most spectacular example is the day Andrea and I flew home to find that the store had burned to the ground. That was insurance claim number one.

Later that year I had some mail and parcels to take to Pan Phillips in the Blackwater. Andrea came with me, and Chuck and Cary stayed home in a house I had built a couple of years earlier. It was Christmas day, and Chuck and Cary were to clean up the mess of opening our presents. The house was heated with a big metal barrel stove, and I guess the two house cleaners filled it with all the wrapping paper and cardboard boxes. The heater got red hot, and when Andrea and I flew back over the Ilgachuz Mountains, all that was left of the house was smoke and ashes and insurance claim number two.

At some point I built a large shed across the road from the store, to store square bales of hay. One day a clerk in the store said something to a customer that was taken the wrong way, and there was a fire, and that was insurance claim number three. We owned a trailer across the road that we rented to a local couple. One day they had a pretty hot party and we were up to insurance claim number four.

. On the C2 Ranch we had a fairly large ranch house that my nephew, Brian Smith, was living in when he took care of the ranch

L to R: Gene Sill with dark glasses, Glen Shortreed, Wes Carter and Bill Graham.

for Wes Carter and me. The house caught fire, apparently because of a short in the wiring, and it burned to the ground. The ranch was in the process of being sold, but the lawyer we had hired drank much too much to be good for him or us, and he had let the fire insurance lapse before the deal was finalized. It should have been claim number five, but we were out of luck. The lawyer died from the excesses of boozing. A bad deal all around.

Airplane insurance also came in handy. One winter day I was landing west of Fort St. James on what was reported to be a hard-packed snow strip. I still had wheels on my plane, as it was too early in the season for skis, and I broke through the snow and the plane landed upside down. I was thankful for the shoulder harness that went with the normal safety belt. I hitched a ride to Fort St. James on a passing ski plane, got in touch with an airplane mechanic I knew in Vanderhoof and turned the repair job over to him. I caught a ride to Anahim Lake, and when I received word that the airplane was repaired and ready to be flown, I went to Vanderhoof to pick it up. On a quick walk-around inspection I noticed

Ken and I enjoy a panoramic view of Ptarmigan Basin in the Itcha Mountains.

the cowling had been cut so the exhaust pipe would fit. I thought this was odd, as it had fit before the accident. I returned to Anahim Lake without any trouble, but the enlarged hole in the cowling didn't sit well with me. I got Slim Shirk, my mechanic and flight instructor from Williams Lake, to look at the plane. He discovered that one of the main engine braces had buckled. This pulled the engine out of line with the airplane, which is why the cowling and exhaust pipe didn't fit properly. I don't believe I paid anything for this repair job. The upside-down plane was probably taken out by helicopter, and the insurance company footed the whole bill.

Twice I snapped off spring-gear landing legs from planes, and twice the insurance paid for it. There is little doubt that to have any peace of mind, you have to have a lot of insurance.

In my last few years in the store business in Anahim Lake, the biggest event of the year besides the annual stampede was our horseback trip to the mountains. Ken Stranaghan, Bob and June Draney, and Kris and I were the main travellers.

Ken would always bring along a treat of fresh crabs and some of his wife's tarts. We always ate the crabs on the first day and

PHOTO KRIS ANDREWS.

left the shells in a conspicuous place along the trail to show other travellers how high on the hog we lived. We always took a liberal amount of booze with us so we could have a drink or two before supper. On one trip we somehow forgot to pack the booze. Luckily Kris had put a bottle of gin in one of the pack boxes. She had purchased this bottle in Mexico and the glass was very weak. When we got ready for our evening drink the first night, we discovered the bottle had broken and the gin was in the bottom of the plastic pack box with our fly spray. We strained the gin, and even under severe rationing we swore that none of us got any insect bites for the rest of the trip.

That was a blessing. When you go riding in the wilderness, things happen that change your outlook, and one of those things is bugs. On one of our mountain rides the horseflies descended upon us so thick you could slap your chaps and kill five or six at a lick. We put as much fly dope on ourselves and our horses as we could, and apparently we no longer smelled like a smorgasbord, because the horseflies took off to find something more to their liking. When horseflies bite they seem to take a chunk out of you and cause a considerable amount of bleeding as well as pain. I guess they are called horseflies because they are particularly attracted to horses.

Another insect can cause even more trouble—the hornet. One summer Kris, Bob, June, Ken and I went riding up to camp at one of Pan Phillips's hunting cabins on the north side of the Ilgachuz. The packhorse in front of me was a tall, good-looking gelding I sometimes rode. As we were going up the last few feet to the cabin, a hornet stung the horse on the belly where the skin is thin and tender. The horse gave such a high and sudden jump that he seemed to explode. The pack stayed on, which we were pretty proud of. I can remember thinking how glad I was that I hadn't been riding the horse.

Years earlier, I was riding home one afternoon when I felt a sudden searing pain on my skull, behind my ear. I knew immediately that it was a hornet. I kept on riding and the pain subsided, but as I rode along I noticed that my right arm and hand were losing their feeling. That was the side I had been stung on, so I started to rub it with my other hand to get the circulation back. That's when I discovered a lump the size of a chicken's egg in my armpit, which must have been cutting off the circulation when my arm was down. So I rode along for a ways with my arm up, and gradually the poison wore off and I got back to normal again.

The mountains we rode in over the years were the Itchas, Ilgachuz, Rainbows, Trumpeter Mountain, the Alplands south of Charlotte Lake, the Kleena Kleene mountains, and the mountains south of Alexis Creek. Our favourite range was the Itchas. They have everything—easy going, good horse feed, easy creek crossings, lots of game and beautiful scenery.

As you ride mountains and the scenery unfolds around you, you get so involved in the pleasure of just being there that all other thoughts are erased from your mind. Many caribou and goats appear on the landscape as you pass by. You catch glimpses of moose and deer, and even the odd grizzly and wolf. Once we came upon a pack of wolves with a fresh caribou kill. There was enough new

Rocky horse trail along Fish Lake, south of Charlotte Lake. We rode in places we shouldn't have, because we knew nothing of the country.

snow to see how the wolves had chased a cow and calf caribou, and when the calf got winded they would duck in and bite it. The calf's heart would have been racing, and we could see by the blood sign in the snow that it would have bled to death after a couple of bites.

Time goes by much faster during a ride than the mind can comprehend. Your stomach, being on a different wavelength, signals that it is time to eat. You stop on some beautiful hillside, and you and the horses have lunch and a rest. That is what riding in the mountains is all about.

Kris and I went into the Itcha Mountains by ourselves for one trip. We were just leaving camp one morning when we heard a lot of noise off in the distance in front of us. About a minute later, a huge flock of sandhill cranes appeared. This crane has to have the noisiest call in the bird world. They found an updraft in front of us and began to circle for altitude—all several hundred of them, and each one was trying to make more noise than the one beside it. These were the survivors of a long summer of raising chicks. Predation by foxes, coyotes, eagles and other animals had no doubt taken its toll. Nature believes that there is safety in numbers and

Kris with horses, ready to start on another mountain ride.

had done a good job on this mass of birds. As they circled in front of us they became layered for room to fly. They continued to circle, seemingly without effort, and kept up their loud cackling until they had reached the right altitude to take off on their migration to the south. It was an exhilarating experience few people have the opportunity to encounter. We were lucky to see it, and extra lucky that they hadn't circled directly overhead, as trail riders don't carry umbrellas.

Sometimes when you are riding in the mountains, you encounter things that your mind just can't comprehend right away. One afternoon in the Rainbow Mountains, Kris and I and Ken Stranaghan were approached by two riders angling into our direction of travel. They were coming very fast but not trotting or galloping. As they got closer we got our first look at a couple of Tennessee Walkers. We met the riders just before we came to a mudhole. They probably didn't know that the Rainbow Mountains are infamous for their nasty little mudholes. To cross muddy places with a horse, you hold him in check so he doesn't punch his feet into the mud and then start lurching to get through it, which can easily cause the horse to bog down and even fall over. We wouldn't be able to overtake the riders to warn them, so we couldn't wait to see what would happen to them in the mud. According to everything I had learned about crossing mud, what they did just shouldn't work. They hit that mudhole going full blast and had no trouble whatsoever. I'm still in wonderment.

I kept my horses at White Meadow, an eighty-acre piece of ground that Wes Carter had bought. Corkscrew Creek ran past the north side of it. There was a nice little cabin on the land and Wes had made a little airstrip on it. White Meadow was very handy for our mountain rides.

In the winter I would feed the horses in a fenced-in area behind the store. I always had a colt or two to work with and a mare to foal in the spring. On the Cless Pocket Ranch we had over a hundred head of horses, which we used to run the ranch. We raised our own draft horses and we always had a workhorse stud. These horses rustled all winter. In the spring we chased them in to the ranch, where the four-year-olds would be cut out and halter-broke and have their feet trimmed. These four-year-olds would seldom have seen a person and were basically wild animals. Every ranch had a round corral with a snubbing post in the middle of it. The horse to be halter-broken was separated from the main bunch and driven into the round corral. It was then roped, and after about a four-hour battle with the aid of the snubbing post, it was halter-broke.

The horses I raised behind the store grew up with me handling them and were very interesting and easy to handle. When I sold the store, I moved to Williams Lake and bought a sizable place on the Horsefly Road and continued to raise a few horses. When you have all the time in the world to handle a horse from the time it is born, it becomes a fantastic animal to work with. About this time a lot of good books and other information came out on how to handle horses. I paid attention to it in teaching my colts all they

Getting to know him.

needed to know for our mountain trips. First I halter-broke them, then I petted them all over so they knew I wasn't going to hurt them, then I picked up their feet until they got used to it. After that I would put a light saddle on the colt and put a snaffle bit in its mouth. Before long the animal would be no stranger to what was going to happen on our trail rides. The more colts I handled, the easier time I had in teaching them what they had to know. I was also learning from them.

I always carried two sets of keys in my pocket, one for the pickup and one for my house. I would take out the wrong set about half the time, so I decided to put my house keys in my left pocket and my car keys in my right pocket. I was still mixing them up weeks later. Then I thought of how much my colts had to learn, and how well they remembered. Once they learned something, they never forgot. I was humbled.

One day Ken Stranaghan and I were moving horses out of White Meadow. We were both mounted and each of us was leading a horse. I was riding a well-broke horse that had been spoiled about creek crossings. At the first crossing we came to, he did a one-eighty, and he would have gone back the way we had come if he'd had his way. I got Ken to hold the horse I was leading and got my horse back to the creek. He tried another one-eighty, and I just petted his neck and assured him everything was all right. When we faced the creek again, I continued to pet his neck and talk to him. This time he crossed. That was the last of his bad habits, and the whole lesson had taken about fifteen minutes. I thought again about my keys.

Another horse I raised, a half-Morgan gelding, had been put through the normal training routine and showed every indication of being a very smart horse. As I was working with other horses at the time, I never seemed to get time to ride him. When it was time for our yearly mountain ride, this horse was three years old and I couldn't wait to take him with us. He was used to the snaffle

D'Arcy and colt: An exercise in trust.

Fording a river with Ken, Kris, June and Bob. If we could have asked for something more, I don't know what it would have been.

bit, so I put him in my little round corral and got on him. He acted like I had done it before. I rode him around for half an hour and repeated it the next day. Now it was time to head for the mountains. We decided to go into the Rainbows, even though some of the creek crossings along the trail didn't have the best of reputations. We trailered our horses to the takeoff point, packed up and took off. Morgans are noted for their strength and endurance, and I could tell my three-year-old was half Morgan. He had never been ridden out of a corral before and had a total riding time of about one hour. I was in the lead of the pack train when we came to a doubtful crossing, and I could easily assure him it was all right to cross. Sometimes I wasn't too sure myself. He totally accepted me as navigator and captain and I trusted him a hundred percent. For a three-year-old horse to respond so well with only a couple of hours' training, absolutely amazed me. I had worked with dozens of horses in my day and had never seen anything comparable. This time I had hit upon a horse that was one in a thousand. We had bonded. We were on the same wavelength.

Kris and I took a drive up to Alaska one year to see the sights and learn a little history. Everything we found out was very interesting, but some was far from our liking. People heading for the gold country a century ago would packhorses as far as they could go on the feed that they could carry. There was no horse feed where they were going, so once they arrived, they would leave the horses to starve to death if they didn't want to waste a bullet. Some more compassionate person wrote a poem to the horse.

Look back at our
Struggle for freedom,
Trace our present day's
Strength to its source,
And you'll find that man's
Pathway to glory
Is strewn with the bones
of a horse.

To get to the Itcha Mountains, Kris and I, Bob and June Draney and Ken Stranaghan would go through Alfred Bryant's old place at Tallywacker. He had guided from there and raised cattle but had sold out and moved to Bella Coola. On one trip, while crossing the meadow we looked toward the Itchas and saw a whitish thread going up a short, steep pitch on the side of a mountain. As we were about twelve miles away, we could only guess what it was, but we decided to take a closer look. The next day we found the mountain and saw that the white thread was a wide band of light-coloured rock going a short distance to the top of a low mountain plateau. It was too steep to ride a horse up, so Ken, Kris and I left our horses with Bob and June and climbed up the light band of rock. We discovered it was a trail the caribou had made by wearing the lichen off the rocks in the line of least resistance to the lush feed on this low mountain. How many caribou had passed over where we were standing and over how many years they had travelled this route, we could only guess. We decided to call it the "caribou stairway to heaven."

This was the second and last time we hunted in the Itcha mountains. We found looking more interesting.

While writing this book I got Kris to see if she could find the trail on Google Earth, and sure enough, there it was, rising fifty-four metres in elevation. Even the coordinates of the trail were given. I found this truly amazing.

♠ JIMMY STILLAS

When Mary Jane Stillas married Mack McEwan, she brought with her a son, Jimmy Stillas, whose father was a Bella Coola Indian named David Moody.

Jimmy was a pretty well-built young fellow of about 180 pounds when I first knew him. The Department of Indian Affairs, under the direction of Bill Christy, the Indian agent in Williams Lake, decided to build a road down the Dean River for the Natives who were ranching there. The Department provided a TD9 International bulldozer and hired the TD6 bulldozer that we used on the Cless Pocket Ranch.

Ulkatcho Chief Jimmy Stillas fastens a spearhead for fishing during the 1987 Tanya Lakes gathering. Jimmy organized gatherings at traditional sites to encourage a resurgence of Native culture. He lived a short influential life and was a great guy. PHOTO SAGE BIRCHWATER.

Jimmy ties his shoes as he and Ulkatcho elder Henry Jack relax and discuss something during the 1990 gathering at Ulkatcho Village. PHOTO SAGE BIRCHWATER.

Mack McEwan and I drove the Cats and Jimmy towed our fuel and camping supplies with a rubber-tired tractor and wagon. The two Cats made a rough road through the bush while Jimmy cleaned up the broken trees and dislodged rocks that we left behind us. I had seldom seen a better worker. He was so absorbed in his work that he hardly ever looked up. I think it rained every day that summer, but it didn't slow Jimmy down.

The next time I saw Jimmy he was loading logging trucks with Ken Stranaghan in Bella Coola, for Crown Zellerbach. One day I had the opportunity to watch him. Jimmy stood on the bulkhead over the cab of the truck and pointed to the log he wanted Ken to get next, the object being to fill the truck without leaving any wasted space on the load. The two men must have been on the same wavelength to even try something like this.

Other local Natives from Anahim Lake were the same—such good workers that they were in big demand for logging. Thomas Yas, Albert Casimir, Oggie Cahoose, Ollie Nukalow and Jimmy

Stillas all performed admirably at their jobs, though every weekend was apparently one unending party. The combination took a heavy toll on them. Thomas and Ollie were killed, Oggie accidentally shot himself to death, Albert lost an eye. Jimmy Stillas survived, but he split up with his wife.

One very cold night in December 1965, I got a call at the store asking to go and help at a house on the reserve. On arriving I could hardly believe what I saw. There had been a shoot-up at a drunken party. Jamos Jack lay dead on the floor, and Sister Suzanne, the resident nurse, was working on Jamos's son, Benny, trying to save his life. Meanwhile the party went on full swing. Jimmy Stillas walked by with a half-empty bottle of wine in his hand, having a hell of a good time. There was no way we could keep the door shut for Sister

Jimmy welcomes Nuxalk elder Clayton Mack, a famous grizzly bear guide and grandson of John Clayton, to the 1987 gathering. Jimmy organized the yearly gathering partly to show that you could still have a good time without drinking. (He had quit some time earlier.) PHOTO SAGE BIRCHWATER.

Chief Jimmy as a happy sober man.

PHOTO SAGE BIRCHWATER.

Suzanne and her patient, as it was about 30 below outside.

The next day I was deputized by the RCMP to go with two police officers and a conservation officer to see if John Sam, who was apparently the shooter, was at his home in Fish Trap. I sat in the back seat of the police car. One officer was driving, another officer sat in the middle with a rifle next to him, and the conservation officer sat by the window. We hadn't driven far when the conservation officer seemed to suddenly become aware of the rifle. He asked whether the gun was loaded, and when he found out it was, he had the driver stop the car and told the other officer that he wasn't allowed to carry a loaded gun in a car. The officer seemed a little confused over this. I know I was. He got out of the car, put the rifle barrel on his foot and ejected all the shells from the gun. If he had accidentally pulled the trigger he would have blown his foot off. When we got to John's house I was much more worried about the company I was in than I was about John Sam. I figured by now he would be sober and wondering how to get out of the mess he was in. He later went to the Nimpo Lake Store and gave himself up to Karl Erickson, the storekeeper, who was a friend of his.

On this horrible night, Jimmy Stillas must have hit rock bottom. He was much too much of a man to continue in a slide like this. With the help of his wife, Olive McInroy, who he lived with on her orchard in Winfield, he quit drinking. This must have been quite a feat after drinking so heavily for so many years. Jimmy then devoted the rest of his life to his people. In 1986 he was elected to the Ulkatcho Band Council, and the next year he was elected chief. He worked untiringly for his band, and among his many accomplishments was his work inviting the mobile alcohol treatment program onto the reserve to work with the community.

Jimmy's favourite way to relax was spending time down the Dean River on his trapline. One day in early November 1990, he went down there to go hunting. He tried to cross a frozen body of water on his snow machine, and unfortunately he broke through the ice. He was knocked unconscious by the impact and he drowned in the cold water. The Ulkatcho First Nation mounted a search once they learned he was missing, and miraculously someone spotted his snow machine tracks from the air, tracks that disappeared into a hole in the ice by a beaver dam. There was a heavy snowfall the next day that would have obliterated any sign of where Jimmy's body was under the ice, and it would have been nearly impossible to find him in that vast wilderness.

Once his body was recovered, he was given every honour his people could bestow upon him. A new education centre on the reserve was named the Jimmy Stillas Learning Centre, and a school at the Nenqayni Wellness Centre near Williams Lake also bears his name. In the few short years Jimmy was chief of the Ulkatcho Nation, he did more to change the lives of his people than had ever been done before.

♠ KEN STRANAGHAN

Ken Stranaghan wasn't an ordinary person by any stretch of the imagination. He was born with an extra glass of champagne in his blood. Ken was just over six feet tall and in his prime was very strong and athletic. He always considered caution to be something for other people.

For a while he looked after the telephone line at the Precipice, east of Anahim Lake, then he went logging for Crown Zellerbach in Bella Coola. He married Jeanette Brynildsen, the granddaughter of Barney Brynildsen, one of the original European settlers in Bella Coola. They had two daughters, Kristy and Diedry.

Ken was a great hunter and sport fisherman. He guided bear hunters at Kwatna, out on the coast west of Bella Coola. In an age where a little liquor was good and lots of liquor was even better, he took a back seat to no one. Once while living at the Precipice, Ken foot-raced a horseback rider down the mountain toward the Atnarko River, a distance of eight or ten miles. I asked him if he had warmed up first and he said he hadn't. In the race he came a close second.

On a hunting trip in the Bella Coola Valley, Ken and his brother-in-law, Don Duncan, shot a moose. They had to get it up a steep hill to their vehicle parked on the road. They quartered the animal, loaded a quarter at a time on Ken's back, and with Don pushing from behind, got the moose to the pickup.

Ken had more lives than a cat and needed every one. When he was falling at Kwatna, he once had a fir log he was bucking pin his leg to the stump. After he got rescued he had to get a metal knee put in. He worked as a faller for a logging company for years out of Bella Coola. Once when he was flying home with a passenger and a dog, he attempted to fly over a mountain pass. He got into a whiteout and crashed into the mountain. Unfortunately the passenger was killed, and the dog was never seen again. Ken was rescued the next day. His head was so swollen he was almost unrecognizable.

Ken fished a lot on the Bella Coola and Atnarko rivers, and was a very skilled boatman on the river. Once he got caught in a logjam and tried to jump out of the boat onto the jam. He landed a little short and grabbed onto a log. The current was so strong he took a deep breath and let go of the log, and was swept under the jam and out the other side. On telling me about this later on, he said he thought he might have drunk half the water in the Bella Coola River.

The champagne in his blood required almost continuous action. This could make for some fine times. I took many memorable mountain trips in different ranges with Ken. But the need for action could also lead to trouble if any sign of boredom reared its

Ken, Bob and me having a reward for virtue at the end of the day on the shores of McKlinchy Lake. PHOTO KRIS ANDREWS.

ugly head. Once when he and Don Duncan were driving down the road having a few drinks, they saw the Department of Highways grader coming up the road. They had a shotgun in the car, and Ken decided they should shoot the exhaust pipe off the grader. This little shoot-up didn't endear them to the driver of the grader, Gordon Levelton. Ken and Don continued down the road to the townsite, where they removed a number of items from the police yard. Better sense finally prevailed and the stuff was returned before they were caught. Ken and Don eventually appeared before the magistrate, Ed Willson. Ken was told he was born a hundred years too late and was fined a hundred dollars. It could have been much worse.

One day at the end of a work shift, Ken, Steve Dorsey, the logging superintendent and the bookkeeper were returning from where they were logging. They got a rowboat to cross the river. Ken threw his lunch kit into the boat first and it popped open, spilling all the nuts and bolts he had taken from the company shop.

Ken, me and Bob Draney. The fat on the caribou shows what great feed was in the Itcha Mountains. PHOTO KRIS ANDREWS.

Anyone else in the world would have been embarrassed at least. Ken made a joke about it and put the booty back in the lunch kit, and they continued across the river.

At one stampede in Anahim Lake it was decided that a cross-country horse race would be held. A swath was cut through the jackpine, down a steep hill, into and across the Dean River and into the rodeo grounds. Ken decided to compete in the race. He picked the horse that my brother-in-law, Slim Brecknock, had won the bareback contest on. Steve Dorsey once said Ken had to live on the edge, and this is what he meant. The horse was finally saddled and positioned by a rider on another horse. No bridle or hackamore was used, as the horse wouldn't know what they were anyway. Ken got into the saddle and told one of the workers to hit the horse over the ass when the race began so he would get a good start. Down a steep hill full of stumps, into and across the Dean River, and into the stampede arena rode Ken on a wild horse that had never been ridden and was running as if the devil was chasing it. Ken was in his element. He won the race.

As the years went by, Ken began to wear out his body. He got very bad headaches, and when the aches and pains got too unbearable he just had another operation. Eventually he had more screws and metal in him than a Volkswagen. His last bad horseback mishap occurred when he was riding with Bill Harestad in the mountains. Ken's horse went over backwards in a bad place and loosened some of the metalworks in his back. With Bill's help he somehow made it to the bottom of the mountain and caught a ride to the hospital. They scheduled him for more surgery, but of course this didn't slow him down. One day he was taking Grant Bittner down the Atnarko River in a rubber raft when it hit a protruding stick in a logjam and flipped over. Grant was able to get to shore, but Ken never surfaced. He went out the way he would have wanted. Some of us on the sidelines were relieved that he didn't wind up in a wheelchair, as we had feared. He could never have stood the confinement.

♠ RICK HANSEN

Rick Hansen, who grew up in Williams Lake, lost the use of his legs in a motor vehicle accident, then travelled around the world in a wheelchair to show people that physical impairment can be overcome. He has raised millions of dollars for spinal cord injury research.

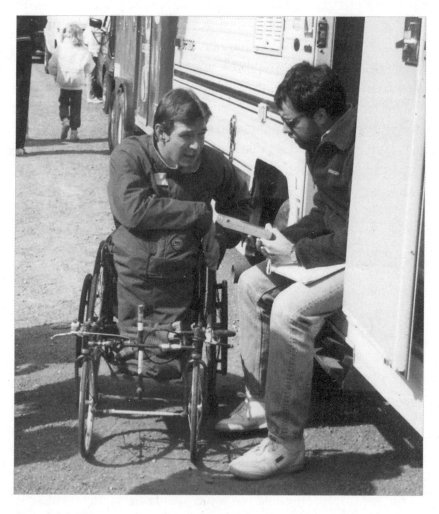

The most important thing I learned from Rick Hansen was this: Don't ever make an excuse if you want to do something.

♠ CHIMPANZEES

Our world is facing a huge quandary. It is not known whether we will end everything with atom bombs or just pollute our nests so badly that we will die in them. In his book *The Third Chimpanzee*, Jared Diamond says that we have 98 percent of the same genes as chimpanzees. Many people in history have had great inspirations. Newton's inspiration came when an apple fell on his head. Mine came when I read we were 98 percent chimpanzee. To settle the world's problems, all we have to do is get that other two percent. I don't suppose I will get the Pulitzer Prize for this, but I do care about saving the world.

♠ SKIING

One of my favourite recreations before the stroke was cross-country skiing. Kris was also fond of skiing, so we planned a ski trip to the Itcha Mountains. We would fly in, and there we would meet Roger and Wanda Williams, and Howard and Janet Prosser.

Everything went as planned and we had a great time skiing on the slopes. By the time we were ready to return to Anahim Lake, it was several degrees below zero. The plane had cooled off and

A group of us skiing in the Rainbow Mountains.

One of my favourite pastimes was cross-country skiing in the mountains.

I flooded the engine trying to get it started. It couldn't be coaxed into starting and I didn't want to wear down the battery, so we decided to get towed down the mountain on our skis behind one of the snow machines, a distance of about fifteen miles.

We came out at Dave and Debbie Altherr's ranch. They had bought the place from Bill and Jane Lehman, and they raised cattle and sheep. I had heard that they had a specially bred dog to watch their flock of sheep, a Hungarian sheep dog known as a Komondor. These dogs weigh well over a hundred pounds, and when one of them is on guard, no coyote or wolf can get near the sheep.

But dogs were the last thing on my mind when we got to the Altherrs' ranch, so as we two skiers were towed past the sheep he was guarding, I was dumbstruck by the sight of the monster dog coming after us full bore. The dog was towing a tire at the end of a rope attached to his collar. He was still being trained and the tire was supposed to act like a tether to keep him from wandering off. That dog came after us so hard and fast that the tire flew behind him, only hitting the ground at intervals. As I turned my head to see if he was going to tear Kris apart, I hit a frozen cowplop with my skis and down I went. Kris fell next to me. We lay entangled in our gear in the snow, with the dog standing over us. From my new vantage point the dog looked as tall as a horse and I half expected that we were about to be torn to shreds. The dog licked Kris's face, then gave me the same greeting, then was gone. Somehow we got back on our skis and continued to the ranch house, where we enjoyed the hospitality of the Altherrs through the evening.

Mack McEwan, Andy Christensen and my cousin John Clayton.

♠ MACK MCEWAN

Freddy McEwan, Mack and Mary Jane McEwan's oldest son, married Jessie Cahoose, one of Gus and Susan's daughters, and they lived at Fish Trap. Freddy was a slow-talking, good-natured, heavy-set guy who in his younger years had a fairly normal thirst for booze. He seemed quite satisfied to keep his senses dulled with drinking, but he always had a sense of humour. One day I was out near the store, shoeing a horse I had just acquired. I had the horse in the angle made by an old log house and a log fence that joined one side of the house. The horse was not happy with what I was doing and was getting a little skittish. Who should wander over to give me moral support and see how I was doing but Freddy McEwan. It was apparent that he had had a snifter or two, or three. He squatted down a few feet behind the horse and started talking to me. I told him that he could find a safer spot to sit, but he seemed to ignore me. The horse got a little more uptight, and then it suddenly pulled back and wheeled around. With a fence on one side and the wall of the cabin on the other the horse had no place to go but over the top of Freddy. I went over to see if he was all right and he said the horse had never touched him. "You just have to know what you're doing," he said.

Fred and Jessie had their share of tragedy. One of their boys drowned in the lake at Fish Trap and another was killed in a car accident. Somewhere along the road the two of them decided to quit drinking, and I'm sure they got rid of a sack full of demons when they did. Fred got a logging truck and hauled logs for years. Maybe he is hauling logs to this day.

♠ ANAHIM LAKE NATIVES

For centuries, the Natives around the Anahim Lake area depended on plentiful local game and fish for sustenance. When the white settlers began to move in, trapping, guiding and working on ranches gave the Natives money for clothing and staples such as sugar, salt and flour. Changes in their daily life came quickly. Fur prices collapsed, ranches became mechanized and displaced their labour, and the government moved families to reserves. Few jobs were available on the reserves, and the land was not always the best real estate to be had. The formerly self-sufficient aboriginal person

The kids were brought in from the surrounding areas to go to the Indian Affairs school (above). In many cases, the parents had nothing to do.
DON & MARILYN BAXTER COLLECTION.

was now a ward of the Crown. He was given a house to live in that he couldn't own, on a piece of property that might be virtually useless.

Josephine Robson left her partner, Louis Squinas, and married Bert Robson. After Bert died, Josephine reunited with Louis.

The future looks much better. The ruling palefaces have determined that the ancestors of the Native people, who lived on this land for centuries in the distant past and who had no use for land title, will now have jurisdiction over vast tracts of the land. As the younger generation of Natives learn to govern themselves with the tremendous responsibility and power that land control has given them, they are beginning to determine their own destiny and to have the opportunity of escaping the rot of welfare.

Most of the Native people I knew and worked with over the years are gone now. My hope is that future generations will never have to face the disruptions they had to face. For their children and grandchildren, the going will not always be calm but they will be the masters of their fate.

♠ POWER FOR ANAHIM

W.A.C. (William Andrew Cecil) Bennett's Social Credit Party easily won the 1966 provincial election, taking thirty-three of fifty-five available seats. It was Wacky Bennett's sixth straight victory. Under his leadership the Socreds had been in power since 1952. In the Cariboo, Bill Speare was elected MLA for the third straight time, but he gave up his seat so that the attorney general, Robert

Very happy BC Hydro officials flank the new Anahim Lake generators. DON & MARILYN BAXTER COLLECTION.

Bonner, could run in a by-election (he had been defeated in the Vancouver–Point Grey riding by the Liberal candidate, Garde Gardom). The Cariboo was considered a safe seat for the Socreds, and Bonner was an important member of Bennett's cabinet, so a by-election was set for the riding in November 1966.

To make sure Bonner would get elected, the Social Credit Party pulled out the stops and sent all kinds of MLAs to the Cariboo to campaign for him. One of them was Isabel Dawson, the MLA for the neighbouring riding of Mackenzie (later called Powell River–Sunshine Coast), which included Bella Coola. The main issue for our community at that time was to get BC Hydro to electrify the area. Most businesses had power plants that were expensive to run, especially in the winter. As more and more people moved into the area, there was a growing need for more and more power. The fishing lodges on Nimpo and Anahim lakes needed power, as did the garages and ranches, and the Indian reserve. The last power plant I had was a 7.5-kilowatt diesel, which cost several thousand dollars new, and you never knew when something would go wrong with it. The one thing you did know was that it was indispensable.

Getting electricity and building the Anahim Lake airport were probably the only two issues that could make the two store owners in Anahim Lake put aside their competition and push together a hundred percent. I was the president of the Anahim Lake Improvement District, and Don Baxter was the secretary-treasurer. We backed the electrification project to the hilt.

As Isabel Dawson campaigned in our area, she probably became aware that the electrification question was the main concern of the vast majority of people in the area. The only way power could be put in was to bring in a couple of big diesel plants and run in power lines. At one meeting, Don Baxter and I got Mrs. Dawson to sign a promise that we would get power if Robert Bonner was elected. Armed with this commitment, Don and I campaigned enthusiastically for Bonner and the Social Credit Party. Bonner won the election after a hard battle.

To put two big generators in the town of Anahim Lake, plus fuel-storage facilities, plus hydro poles and transmission lines, was going to be a huge job. After the election, weeks went by, and weeks turned into months, and still no word from our new MLA about our power plant. Considering the reputation politicians have with broken promises, I was beginning to have my doubts. As Harold Engebretson once said during a campaign, about a political candidate he didn't like, "Get him elected then we'll never see him again."

Harold Engebretson: A man with some funny, deep thoughts.

With Don Baxter as secretary and me as president of the Anahim Lake Community Association, we were able to put a lot of pressure on "the forces that be" to get an airport and electricity in Anahim Lake.

DON & MARILYN BAXTER COLLECTION.

As time wore on, I thought of the time my former poker partner, Ollie Nukalow (Johnny Robertson), was called up for the armed forces. He had to go to a screening centre near Vancouver. For a man who had lived his life in the bush, this must have been quite intimidating. He got on a bus and found his way to his destination. I guess the authorities soon determined that Ollie would be of greater value to the war effort by staying at home and working on a ranch in Anahim Lake than by serving in the army. One of the stories he told about his adventure was about running into a fellow on the street who asked him if he could borrow a few dollars. He said he only needed the money until the banks opened and he would meet Ollie right there in two hours and pay him back. Ollie dug up a few dollars for the guy, and two hours later he went to the meeting place. "This guy must be forget where he supposed to meet me," Ollie told me later. "I wait a long time, still he no comin'."

Feeling quite sure that we were waiting in vain for our power plant, I wrote a letter to the *Williams Lake Tribune* telling how Mrs. Dawson had signed a campaign promise for our BC Hydro power, and that maybe she had forgotten where she was when she made the promise, as we hadn't heard from her since the election. I mailed the letter, and the next day I learned that we were going to get our power plant after all. Luckily the mail was slow and the newspaper only came out once a week. I phoned the *Tribune* and asked them not to publish the letter.

Two years later the work was done. In 1969, two big 150-kilo-watt diesel generators were installed at Anahim Lake, and power lines were strung as far as Nimpo Lake. We had our power.

♠ SPORTS

People growing up in small communities don't have much opportunity to engage in sports. Carey Price, who grew up in Anahim Lake and was drafted fifth overall in 2005 by the Montreal Canadiens, was one great exception. Where I grew up in Bella Coola and Anahim Lake, most people worked long hours, leaving little time for much else. All communities required a hall for meetings, dances, etc., so basketball became popular. Softball was another easy game to play without too much infrastructure.

When I finally decided to try cross-country skiing, I was well over thirty. I enjoyed it very much but didn't have the time or the youth to get very skilled at it. When I started downhill skiing, I was definitely a little long in the tooth for it.

On one of the first days I tried skiing, I went with my son, Chuck. He had never skied before either. We went to the old ski hill about ten miles north of Williams Lake toward Quesnel, and we were laboriously making our way down the hill when we came to a short, steep hill. As we stood there wondering how to get down it, two girls came whizzing by, and as they passed us they both curled a ski up behind them and went down the hill on one ski each. I think this is when I learned what the word *macho* meant.

Kris started skiing a little late too. One winter day she and I went skiing up at a hill in Quesnel. We were not having an easy time in our descent, and someone yelled from the chairlift for us to only turn our legs and keep our bodies facing down the hill. This not only showed how green we were, but with a little practice it also helped our skiing immensely.

Chuck and I bought a condo in Nancy Greene's lodge at Sun Peaks outside of Kamloops, and a few years back, a few of us

Fishing in the Itcha Mountains. Two caribou came up behind me when Kris was taking this picture but she didn't have time to take a picture of them before they ran off.   PHOTOS KRIS ANDREWS (ABOVE AND RIGHT).

Fishing with my granddaughters, Sydney and Megan, in Corkscrew Creek.

stayed there for a weekend. I wound up skiing in a group with Nancy Greene leading the way. She was such a good skier and won so many races that she was named Canadian athlete of the year. When we came to some steeper going and rougher terrain, for some reason Nancy asked me if I was sure I wanted to follow her. All I said was that I was sure I could get to the bottom. I didn't explain how I was going to accomplish it. Our group finally wound up back at the bottom of the hill. The next day Chuck, Kris and I were getting ready to play golf when Nancy came by. The course had just been built and was pretty rough, so she was concerned about us losing balls there, and she asked if I had any old balls. I said I had a couple about fifty-five years old. She just smiled and we went our different ways. From these few encounters, I came to the conclusion that the continued limelight had not adversely affected a very down-to-earth lady.

One foggy morning on the Sun Peaks hill, I came to a divide in the run. I could go either of two ways, the Face or the Chute. The Chute sign caused warning bells to go off in my head. I knew what a chute was. Three other fellows were in the process of going down this run, so I stopped to watch. Two of them had paused about fifty feet down the hill, where they were giving explicit instructions to the third skier on where he should land when he started his descent. Where they were going looked like goat country to me. Had I chosen the Chute, the only way I would have got down alive would have been with a parachute.

♠ HUNTING

Old Cahoose from Ulkatcho Village produced five boys, Joe, George, Gus, Andrew and Tommy. Stanley Cahoose, a grandson of Andrew, was a young fellow with no particular desire to achieve

Old Joe Cahoose in a contemplative pose at Tanya Lakes. Taken in 1987.

PHOTO SAGE BIRCHWATER.

too much. One fall he went on a hunting trip as a guide's helper in the mountains down the Dean River. Their hunter had got his moose and they had packed it out about six miles when the hunter realized he had left his camera back where he had killed the moose. It was late in the day, so Stanley hurried back. He had to cross a creek along the way, and the horse stumbled and Stanley got soaked. Darkness fell, and the trail was too rough to travel at night. Stanley's matches were wet so he couldn't light a fire, so he took the saddle off his horse and

Ulkatcho elder Andy Cahoose looking for fish to gaff. PHOTO SAGE BIRCHWATER.

prepared to spend a cold night on the trail. Late fall gets very cold in this country. When he told me the story later, I said, "I guess that was a long night, eh Stan." He replied, "No. I lean into the padding of the saddle and put my saddle blanket over me. I go to sleep. When I wake up the sun he's way high in the sky. I have to hurry back to catch those other guys." Not many palefaces that I know could sleep like that under those circumstances.

♠ LOG HOUSE BUILDING

In the early years, most white settlers in Bella Coola and elsewhere on the coast built houses out of lumber, as it was readily available. In the Interior, almost all the early buildings were made of logs.

The first log cabins were weatherproofed by forcing moss between the logs. My brother-in-law, John Brecknock, once asked me what the old-timers used for chinking and I told him twisted coyote turds. On close examination this seemed quite plausible, but I doubt that there were enough coyotes. Eventually John found out I was only kidding.

For a time, mud was tried out as insulation, but mud dried out and cracked, causing air leakage. Then builders began to scribe their logs so they would fit more tightly, and the top log was grooved and placed down over a strip of insulation laid down the length of the bottom log. When fibreglass insulation became available, this method worked very well.

For a long while, roofs were made of poles nailed on stringers as close together as they could get, and covered with sod. Eventually poles were split in half and placed on the stringers, split side up with sod on top. Enough lumber could be whipsawed to make doors, windows and floors. In whipsawing, one man worked the saw standing in a pit below the log, and one man worked from above on a platform over the log. This was a miserable job. Over time, small sawmills started up and lumber became more fashionable. Off the beaten track, logs were still in use until most people had moved to small towns. When lumber was the main material, a big change came about—indoor plumbing became common. It was the end of outdoor toilets and Eaton's catalogues.

♠ THE TRUTH ABOUT LUCK

One morning in 2002, as I was getting mobile after a night's sleep, I took a step away from the end of the bed and landed flat on the floor like a ton of bricks. Not having a clue what happened, I somehow got to my feet and tried another step. Same result.

Kris was downstairs, and the sound of me falling startled her enough that she ran upstairs to see what was going on. I was lying on the floor and told her my legs wouldn't work. She said I had had a heart attack and phoned for an ambulance. I was eventually medevaced to Kamloops. The verdict was I'd had a stroke.

A pacemaker was the answer to my problems. I couldn't eat

The source of luck is family: Cary, Andrea, Chuck and me, along with Cary's two daughters, Sydney and Megan.

for twenty-four hours before the operation, and meanwhile I had developed unstoppable hiccups. After the operation I was allowed to eat but had to lie on my back. Between that and the hiccups, I thought I was going to choke on my food. It turned out that one of the leads from my pacemaker to my heart wasn't in the right place, and another operation was scheduled. I told the staff about my trouble with the hiccups and a nurse volunteered to stop them. She got a syringe and jammed the needle into my upper arm. I had never felt a needle like that before. I could have sworn it was a four-inch nail that she shoved in until it hit the bone. If I were a woman I would have fainted, if I were a horse I would have given the nurse both hind feet, but being a man I had to just stand there and take it. The nurse then injected the contents of the syringe. This must have consisted of rattlesnake venom—every drop burned like fire.

The second operation was a hundred percent effective, and in a month I was able to walk again.

This was different from any other time I had been sick or hurt.

Once when Kris and I were skiing at Jasper, we were heading down an easy slope when a skier fell in front of me. I got around her by the skin of my teeth, but fell as I went by. I landed on the camera in my pocket, which didn't hurt the camera but raised hell with my ribs. When it takes five minutes to roll over and get out of bed, you know you have broken ribs. Years ago the treatment was to bind that part of your body with tape, but now broken ribs are left to heal on their own. I sneezed once during the healing time and would never do that again. For a few seconds it was absolutely agonizing. I learned that broken ribs behave better when you're vertical than when you're horizontal. I also learned that when you make the wrong move, the pain immobilizes you.

How could I resist having my picture taken here? PHOTO KRIS ANDREWS.

A few years later, I got into rib trouble again. I was breaking a young horse behind the store, leading it across a creek in a pasture. I had a little collie that was my constant companion. He would bring my hat when I asked him, he knew a lot of tricks and he helped me move cattle. He was just a dandy little dog. On this occasion he didn't think my horse was moving fast enough, so with me in the lead and the horse following, my little helper nipped the horse in the hock. Neither the horse nor I was expecting it, and when the horse jumped, one knee hit me just off my backbone and sent me flying. I knew I was in for broken rib syndrome again, for a month or more.

Like Napoleon, I like to seize the high ground.

One fall Kris and I decided to visit Las Vegas. One of the first things we saw was the Cirque du Soleil show at Treasure Island. We had breakfast on the Strip in the morning, and the plan was that Kris would go shopping and I would go back to the Mirage, where we were staying, and play poker. I walked her to the shops, and then I started feeling very peculiar. I didn't say anything to Kris, I just started back to the Mirage. I hadn't gone half a block when I knew I was in trouble. My body almost quit working. I wondered if I had got ptomaine poisoning from breakfast. I could see the big Mirage sign but didn't know if I could get to it. I would go a little way and lean on anything I could find for a rest. All I wanted to do now was to get to my room, and after a tough trek I finally reached it. I had only been there a few minutes when the pain hit me. It was so bad I just kept throwing up. Kris finally came back from shopping and realized I must be very sick if it had kept me from playing poker. We phoned the front desk, but there was no doctor in the hotel. We got a taxi to take us to a clinic, and even though it was jammed full of people waiting, the staff took one look at me and got me in to see the doctor. Apparently there are only two things that can cause pain like that: kidney stones or gallstones. The doctor diagnosed kidney stones, then gave me a shot of Demerol and I was hooked up to an IV. By now I was completely dehydrated, so this was one of the best meals I ever had.

My urine was strained in Vegas and again in Williams Lake when we got back home. Nothing was ever found. I still can't understand how something that couldn't be found could stop my body from working even before the pain hit. I'm glad that it has never come back.

Before the stroke, these were the most serious health problems I had run into. The only lasting effect was something out of kilter after the second time I broke some ribs. Things are different now. My left side can't tell hot from cold, my balance is bad and my sneezer was adversely affected. I haven't sneezed for eight years. The balance problem curtailed my activity with horses and of course all riding in the mountains. My tether has been shortened considerably, but compared to other stroke victims I have seen, I was very lucky.

With many of my former activities curtailed by the stroke, I turned more to poker for entertainment. Local poker is not just about winning money, although that helps. It is also about outmanoeuvring different people that you are playing against. This quite often happens in such a way that everybody at the table gets a good laugh, as when the best hand loses to a miracle catch by a worse hand (donkeying), or a player steals a pot by betting and driving the other player out of the pot when holding a worse hand.

There is always an undercurrent of amusement in the local games. With a certain amount of tension in a poker game, laughter comes easily, probably as a natural way of breaking tension.

I will tell of a few players I play with, and any similarity in their names to the names of actual living or dead people is just coincidental. There is Tom and Jan (hostess extraordinaire), who just don't like to lose. If they do lose they are always able to dig up a few

In the Itcha Mountains, where you cannot be bored by the scenery.

PHOTO KRIS ANDREWS.

dollars for the next games out of their vast supply of wealth. Their daughter Kayla has just about quit playing with us. Apparently she has found boys more interesting.

There is Ron Two-Feathers, Bev and Ashley. They are three tough players. Ron lives to donkey some player out of a pot. The room is seldom without the music of Bev's laughter. There is Frank the Paleface, who drinks a case of Coke a day and is a menace to sit beside. Frank the Native will throw a big bet at you and then stare at you like he's going to scalp you. Albert and his wife Kayleen are good quiet players who are also good to each other. They are expecting twins. Dennis is in a wheelchair, not because of poker. He does well for a newcomer and has a snappy rebuttal for any lip that might go his way. Jody likes to enlarge the betting on occasion and can be a tough customer. The heavies are Mica, Archie and

Randy. They are three big jolly guys. Randy and Mica just have to look at each other to produce loud laughter. Steve is normally a cautious player but is not above trying to steal a pot, and so is his son Rolly. Bob seems to win more than his share of tournaments. I nicknamed him All-In Bob. Ronnie Two-Whiskers sits in a game like Kawliga until he wins a big pot, then he lights up like a Christmas tree. Joe comes out with a rare funny joke, but mainly waits 'til the iron is hot before attacking. I've seen Shaun Davis put on a poker seminar when getting terrible cards that would have to be called professional. Chuck knows more about card and pot odds than there are grains of sand on all the beaches in the world. Andrea can play tough poker and wins her share but thinks the game is evil when she gets a bad beat. Elder statesman Fred is hard to put on a hand because half the time he doesn't know what he's got. Troy is extremely careful not to buy into a tournament for too much. He makes so much money as an electrician he can't even count it. Vern runs the show through the government and does a great job and obviously enjoys doing it.

Recently Chuck, Andrea and I attended tournaments in Edmonton where Chuck and Andrea both placed, and I had the best streak of winning cards in my life. The poker god sat on my shoulder when I won ninth place in one tournament and finished second in two other tournaments. It makes sense that three people have three times as much chance of winning as one but, somehow, having my kids with me has always made me feel lucky. Any day now I will win the big one.

ACKNOWLEDGEMENTS

I AM MOST GRATEFUL FOR THE EXCELLENT SERVICES PROVIDED BY Sage Birchwater and his company *All Things Write*: communicating between the publisher and myself, finding and refining many pictures for the book and researching the history of specific events and characters in my story.

I would also like to thank my partner Kris Andrews for her uncomplaining help in sending information to the publisher via the computer.

The horses that were raised and taught to carry us through the mountains were much appreciated. Without them the mountain trips would not have been made.

A special thanks to Vici Johnstone, Patricia Wolfe and Michelle Winegar at Caitlin Press for their help in getting this book published. Thanks to Mary Schendlinger for editing the various drafts of the manuscript and getting it right for the publisher.

I would also like to add a special acknowledgment to the late Vern Ashley. Vern was a fine poker player who ran a small tournament in his pool hall, and by his honest and commanding personality made it into a social event that did much to cement good relations and understanding between the aboriginal and white communities. Though bent over by excruciating back problems, he stood tall and straight to those that knew him.

INDEX

MORE GREAT READS BY CAITLIN PRESS

Whitewater Devils: Adventure on Wild Waters, Jack Boudreau
Adventure/Local History ISBN 978-1-894759-46-5, 6 x 9, 256 pp, pb, b&w photos, $22.95

Trappers and Trailblazers, Jack Boudreau
Adventure/Local History ISBN 978-1-894759-39-7, 6 x 9, 256 pp, pb, b&w photos, $22.95

Sternwheelers and Canyon Cats, Jack Boudreau
Adventure/Local History ISBN 978-1-894759-20-5, 6 x 9, 256 pp, pb, b&w photos, $18.95

Wild & Free, Frank Cooke, as told by Jack Boudreau
Local History ISBN 1-894759-04-4, 6 x 9, 272 pp, pb, b&w photos, $24.95

Jacob's Prayer, Lorne Dufour
Local History/Memoir ISBN 978-1-894759-33-5, 5.5 x 8, 160 pp, pb, b&w photos, $18.95

North of Iskut: Grizzlies, Bannock and Adventure, Tor Forsberg
Local History/Memoir ISBN 978-1-894759-42-7, 6 x 9, 216 pp, pb, b&w photos, $24.95

Edge of the Sound: Memoirs of a West Coast Log Salvager, Jo Hammond
Local History/Memoir ISBN 978-1-894759-49-6, 6 x 9, 256 pp, pb, b&w photos, $24.95

Surveying Northern British Columbia: A Photo Journal of Frank Swannell,
Jay Sherwood
Local History/Biography ISBN 1-894759-05-2, 10.5 x 10.5, 166 pp, pb, b&w photos, $29.95

The Railroader's Wife: Letters from the Grand Trunk Pacific Railway,
Jane Stevenson
Local History/Railroad ISBN 978 1-894759-43-4, 6 x 7, 196 pp, pb, b&w photos, $24.95

This Vanishing Land: A Woman's Journey to the Canadian Arctic, Dianne Whelan
Travel/Adventure ISBN 978-1-894759-38-0, 8 x 9, 176 pp, pb, b&w photos, $28.95

call: 1 877 964 4953 or visit:

caitlin-press.com